GETTING

BETTER
WITH AGE

IMPROVING MARKETING
— *in* —
THE AGE OF AGING

PETER HUBBELL

GETTING

BETTER
WITH AGE

IMPROVING MARKETING
in
THE AGE OF AGING

PETER HUBBELL

LONDON   NEW YORK   SHANGHAI
MADRID   BARCELONA   BOGOTA
MEXICO CITY   MONTERREY   BUENOS AIRES

Published by
LID Publishing Inc.
31 West 34th Street, Suite 7004,
New York, NY 10001, US

info@lidpublishing.com
www.lidpublishing.com

A member of:

BPR
Business Publishers Roundtable

www.businesspublishersroundtable.com

© Peter B. Hubbell 2015
© LID Publishing Inc. 2015

Printed in the United States
ISBN: 978-0-9860793-1-3

Cover designer: Chris Baffa
Text designer: Caroline Li

TABLE OF CONTENTS

FOREWORD: *The Good Old Days by Tim Love*   IX

PREFACE   XIII

INTRODUCTION   XVII

PART ONE: *Aged to Perfection*

CHAPTER ONE:
Living in the Age of Aging   03

CHAPTER TWO:
We Have Become Them   11

CHAPTER THREE:
Aging Is the Future of Living   17

CHAPTER FOUR:
Living in the Moment   25

CHAPTER FIVE:
Fuelling the Longevity Economy   33

CHAPTER SIX:
The Old Rush is Underway   41

PART TWO: *Things that Get Better with Age*

CHAPTER SEVEN:
Wine   49

CHAPTER EIGHT:
Leather   57

CHAPTER NINE:
Cheese   65

CHAPTER TEN:
Memories   73

CHAPTER ELEVEN:
Cast-Iron Skillets   83

PART THREE: *Fifty Ways to Get Better with Age*

- *Everything Big Starts Small*   95
- *Age Is Not a Number or Color*   97
- *Break Free from the Inertia of Success*   101
- *Get Off the Stationary Bike*   105
- *Cross the Line*   107
- *Sell Umbrellas When It Rains*   111
- *Do It with Feeling*   115
- *Beware the Generational Abyss*   119
- *Take Flying Lessons*   123
- *Look For The Red Flags That You Can't See*   127
- *Help Them Reimagine*   131
- *The Secret to Success Is Knowing the Secrets*   135
- *Have an Insight for Insights*   139
- *Live the Golden Rule of Marketing To Age:
  There Is No Silver Bullet*   143
- *Speak their Language – Words Matter*   147
- *Get Ahead by Getting Started*   151
- *See the World the Way They See It*   155
- *Revelation, Not Revolution*   157
- *Win at the Edges*   161
- *Only the Names Have Been Changed*   165
- *Grant Them Permission*   169
- *There's Joy in Aging (Really)*   173
- *Create Depth with Layers*   177
- *Create Timeless Ideas for Ageless People*   181

- *Differentiate Between Life and Living*   185
- *Consult Your Doctor If You Think You May Have Boomeritis* 189
- *Don't Cut the Tail Off the Dog*   193
- *Wisdom Gets Better with Age*   197
- *Make Hay While the Sun Shines*   199
- *Don't Market to their Maladies*   203
- *Get the New News on Old Habits*   207
- *Airplane Mode?*   211
- *Strategy Is about Choices – Choice Helps You Win*   213
- *Act Your Age*   217
- *Be Popular By Understanding The Pop Culture Of Aging*   221
- *Know When To STOP*   225
- *Don't Let the Digital Tail Wag the Idea Dog*   229
- *Target Values to Create Value*   233
- *Make Sure your Marketing Hits "Home"*   237
- *Use the Right Tool for the Job*   243
- *Quality Matters*   247
- *Live Fast, Die Old*   251
- *Luck Is a Strategy*   255
- *Make Human Contact: Replace Online with On-Live*   259
- *Learn Something New from Ancient Wisdom*   263
- *The Next Emerging Market Is Not on the Map*   267
- *Consumers Don't Know What They Want until They Do*   271
- *Go Beyond Brand Loyalty to Brand Belonging*   277
- *Look for Trends within the Trends*   281
- *Life Cannot Be Judged until It Is Complete*   285

AFTERWORD   289

RECOMMENDED READINGS   293

ABOUT BOOMAGERS   297

NOTES   299

FOREWORD
By Tim Love

THE GOOD OLD DAYS

I learned a lot about being old when I was young. Back in 1972, this kid from Ohio pointed himself towards the canyons of Madison Avenue to start an advertising career at a venerable agency then known as Dancer Fitzgerald Sample. My first assignment was to work with the agency's Procter and Gamble client, and after only a few weeks on the job, my supervisor asked me to attend a big meeting in Cincinnati. As a lowly Assistant Account Executive, my job was to carry the large portfolio bag of storyboards, to listen, to learn and, most of all, to keep quiet.

These were the days now immortalized as the "Mad Men" era, so the meeting necessitated a long dinner the night before in Cincinnati between our team and the client team. As I was doing my best to keep quiet during the dinner, the founder of our agency, Cliff Fitzgerald, sauntered up puffing a large cigar. He greeted our table warmly and my supervisor introduced me as 'the new man at the agency working on P&G.' Mr. Fitzgerald and I shook hands when he abruptly asked, "Say, would you like to meet Red Deupree?"

I sheepishly asked who was Red Deupree? He replied: "Well, he's the former Chairman and CEO of The Procter and Gamble Company and I am having dinner with him in this restaurant tonight."

Without waiting for an answer, Mr. Fitzgerald beckoned me to follow him across the restaurant to a large, corner table of men, all tucking into giant steaks and conversing through a thick haze of cigar smoke.

Mr. Richard Redwood Deupree (known as "Red" to only a few close friends, including President Eisenhower) was the first non-Procter or Gamble family member named to lead P&G. He became President/CEO in 1930 at the start of the Great Depression and led the Company through these difficult times and throughout World War II. He relinquished the President title in 1948 to become Chairman of the Board, a position he held until 1959.

Meeting Red Deupree was exceptional for many reasons, notably because of his legendary accomplishments as one of the most tenured of all P&G leaders, but also because of his age.

He was by far the oldest person I had ever seen in my life up to that point, so old, it took my breath away. Mr. Fitzgerald introduced me, "Red, this is Mr. Tim Love, our newest recruit working on your business."

I reached out to shake Mr. Deupree's frail hand. He glanced up and motioned to me to lean in. He took my hand, looked me hard in the eye and emphatically said, "Just build the business. Just build the business." That was it.

This is the imprint that I had on aging as I entered the marketing services business as a baby boomer at the green age of 23. In 1972 the advertising industry was heavily focused on appealing to my generation because it was the largest demographic group in the history of the Country. If you could win over 80 million of what became called the "Baby Boom Generation", fortunes could literally be made overnight. As the Boomers aged into and through the 18-49 year-old target market, this paradigm remained unchanged for my next 40 years in the business.

Today, this generation of consumers is still the most valuable generation due not only to its size, but also to its disproportionate amount of disposable income and purchasing power. Due to improved life expectancy and lower birth rates, this generational cohort will continue to dominate demographics for years to come both in the US and abroad.

This shifting context for advertising and marketing communications presents an opportunity to better serve the needs of those who are now 50+ years of age and entering a new life stage. This consumer change-point demands new insights, ideas and brand reassessment for better serving their needs. From healthcare, to investment strategy, certainly, but even beyond that to understanding how this population uses new communication technology, views fashion, perceives beauty, food, beverages and more.

Now wiser for a lifetime of experience, I am still finding new meaning in my first impression those many years ago with Mr. Deupree. My perception of what old is (and is not) has clearly changed, but my belief in the importance of "Just build the business" has remained as steadfast as a rock. Deupree once said, "Nothing is complicated. If it's complicated, don't do it. It must be simple to perform."

Recently I Googled Richard R. Deupree to see if he really was as old as he looked in my memory. That evening in 1972 he was 87 years old. By today's standards, and my own relative age, 87 doesn't seem as old now. If you adjust for today's life expectancy, his 87 would be the same as today's 102. Red was still as sharp as a tack at 102.

The message here is simple. "Old" isn't what it used to be, for me, and for marketers. In fact, there's a big future in age, as evidenced by the existence of BoomAgers, an advertising agency dedicated to the aging consumer marketplace. Founded by advertising veteran Peter Hubbell, BoomAgers has been helping some of the world's top marketers to better understand aging and to adjust their perception of what "old" really is.

Peter's perspective on this opportunity is well articulated in his first book on the subject—*"The Old Rush."* In his latest work herein, Peter provides inspiring insights based on his agency's first-hand experience from working with aging consumers from all corners of the aging world. *"Getting Better with Age"* is an invaluable source of perspective and advice that will help you unlock the secrets to success in marketing to the highly valuable generation of baby boomer consumers.

As I approach an age much closer to what I had defined as old age when I was young, I can attest to the fact that many things in life do in fact get better with age. To prove it to my generation as they get less spry and more gray – and to the younger generations of marketers who need to understand us - I am working with BoomAgers to capture these real life "aphorisms of age" in a future sequel called *"The Book That Gets Better With Age."*

Looking back, it is only now that I understand what Bob Dylan meant in his 1967 song, "My Back Pages:"

> "Ah but I was so much older then.
> I'm younger than that now."

TIM LOVE
Former Vice Chairman Omnicom Group and
Chief Executive Officer; Omnicom – Asia Pacific, India,
Middle East & Africa.

PREFACE

If you live long enough to experience much of the real world, nothing should surprise you anymore. While I more than qualify on the first two requirements, it bewilders me that I'm still surprised by many things, particularly human nature. As a marketer, I am a master at understanding and predicting people's behavior, yet all too often, real human truth eludes the seeker. So I keep at it, ever-vigilant for a glimpse of insight while remaining girded for a surprise.

In my role as an advertising agency CEO and aging consumer expert, I'm blessed to spend time with some of the smartest marketers in the world. They're smart because they're intelligent, well-trained leaders, but also because they're shrewd enough to opportunistically seek the wisdom of an expert to help them gain a critical edge in the marketplace. They've made it to where they are because they have an instinctual knack for figuring things out and then acting on them. These are not people who should be surprised by facts, so imagine how surprised I am when they are.

As I travel the world and speak to smart people about aging, the observation that surprises them most is that there is joy in aging – there's scientific evidence that people actually get happier as they get older. Their reaction is one of incredulity. "How could this be? Sheer nonsense. Poppycock."

People do in fact get happier as they age, mostly because they have arrived at a new stage. Gone are the years of striving and providing, replaced instead with years in which aging people are able to reflect on a life well lived and enjoy a calming contentedness in who they are. All the lessons gleaned from their lifetime of experiences have created wisdom and competence that has them brimming with confidence about life's new possibilities.

The main reason so many smart marketers are surprised by this insight is that too many of them have yet to live the life of the aging consumer. As smart as they are, they lack − through no fault of their own − a first-hand understanding of what it feels like to be older. They're experts at marketing to consumers aged 18 to 34 because they've personally been there, done that. But when it comes to an aging consumer, they simply don't know what they don't know.

The other reason they're surprised is that most of them are rational thinkers. The happiness and optimism that most aging people are feeling is driven by an emotional or irrational reaction to the rational reality of aging (more on that later). When a rational mind-set is confronted with a "fact" that's irrational, incomprehension ensues.

If it's indisputable that we live in the Age of Aging − that global cultures and economies are being transformed by the unprecedented aging of the world's population − then it's time to get real about the reality that's reshaping the landscape of global markets. Someone or something has to help marketers comprehend the incomprehensible truths of global aging.

For the time being, I am that someone, and this book is the something that endeavors to bring clarity and insight to what is simultaneously one of the most valuable but least understood and least leveraged opportunities in marketing. If the Most Valuable Generation™ in the history of marketing believes that they're getting better with age, then we need to get better at marketing to age.

This won't be easy, but then again nothing truly worth pursuing ever is. As compelling and lucrative as marketing to age is and will be, it represents a change to the norms of marketing, and all change must overcome the powerful inertia of the status quo. In this instance, the status quo is our cultural orientation to aging and marketing's bias toward a consumer aged 18 to 49.

Our culture covets new, and young is infinitely preferred to old. We've gone from being an economy where people once made the things they needed and repaired them when they were broken, to today's disposable economy, where old things are enthusiastically replaced with new things well before they're obsolete. In fact, we are so infatuated with new that many of us spend too much time chasing the newest new thing. (Who are those people who stand in line overnight to be the first ones to get the newest iPhone?)

Then there are the marketers who have always believed that a younger consumer is more valuable than an older one, a mind-set created and perpetuated by marketing's original love affair with the Boomers. While the Boomers were searching for the meaning of life, Madison Avenue found meaning in their magnitude – 80 million strong – when the first of them turned 18 in 1964 and created the media target audience of 18- to 49-year olds that would define most of marketing's best practices for the ensuing three decades as the Boomers came of age. All of the industry's philosophies, processes, and practices have been optimized around an age 18-49 orientation, and the inertia is substantial.

Getting Better With Age takes a big step forward in reconciling the discrepancy between progress and inertia by helping you to persevere in a changing world. It will hopefully surprise you in all the ways that surprises can be delightful, and delight you in all the ways that enlighten. If I succeed at expressing all of my deeply felt passions for this topic, I will have created words that inform you with insight and inspire you to action. Done well, these will be the elusive words and understanding that will help you interpret aging consumers' human nature so you can speak their language in a way that opens their hearts. Wouldn't that be a nice surprise?

Finally, and as always, I am grateful for all the circumstances and supportive friends that have provided me with the perspective that gives my life meaning; for the opportunity to grow up on a farm and learn the value of hard work; for the chance to create great advertising work for so many wonderful client partners for so many years; to my father, who taught me that the best way to live a long life was to live one day at a time; to my mother, who believes in me more than I believe in myself; and to my dear wife Caroline and family, who understand that all my long hours of work are actually all about preserving our quality time.

Special thanks in this endeavor also go to the best business partner I've ever had – John Bowman – for his omnipresent wit and inspirational advice, and to Michael Tive, my publishing consultant, who prodded me to keep everlastingly at it by actually believing that the impossible was possible.

PETER B. HUBBELL

INTRODUCTION

I recently visited my doctor for my annual health exam, and while I was enduring the customary wait in the reception area, I noticed that the plaque on the wall that used to read Preventative Health Care had been replaced by one promising Life Extension. What I used to think I needed had been replaced by what it was that I had really wanted all along – some assurance of a longer life. Suddenly, I was seeing wellness with a whole new optimistic lens. Tell me what I want to hear – I'm a Baby Boomer, aren't I?

Yes, we are all living longer, with a determination to live better than the generations that have preceded us. In our country's last 100 years, we've added 30 years to average life expectancy, which is now 78 years of age. If we use current demographic measures to extrapolate for the next 100 years, we are on course to extend our longevity an additional 20 years by 2099 – a possibility that is almost inconceivable.

In that the world's aging population is living a quantity and quality of life that are totally unprecedented, they are free to make up new rules as they go. As such, the challenge for those of us who lead consumer-facing businesses is to apply a corresponding set of new rules to our long-established practices to ensure that our offerings stay relevant in a demographically dynamic world. Global aging is real and it's irreversible. The old way of doing things won't work with an aging consumer. It's time to rethink the way we think.

Metacognition is the psychological term for our awareness and ability to influence our own thinking or, in short, thinking about how we think. If you were a mechanic, metacognition would be more familiar to you as "troubleshooting". Imagine a car that has been brought to a mechanic because it keeps stalling. At face value, his job is to fix the engine, but when he goes past the solution to think more comprehensively about the problem, he might fix the engine problem simply by replacing some bad gasoline.

The essential ambition of *Getting Better With Age* is to get you to think differently about aging; to put aside what you think you know and bring an open mind to learning more about what's really going on in the minds of the aging consumer. If you can understand how they think, the vision for success will become crystal clear.

Part One – Aged to Perfection – provides a foundational understanding of the aging of marketing's Most Valuable Generation™. While the demographic facts of global aging are clear, what's less obvious is the relationship between the physical and psychological aspects of aging. While medical science posits that an aging person is a person in decline, the soul and spirit of this ageless generation keeps propelling them to a limitless future. They aren't getting old, they're *growing* old by reimagining their lives, living in the moment, and staying vital. In light of their massive numbers, this new dynamic of aging is doing more than just inspiring new lifestyles, it's fueling a longevity economy. With so many Boomers exiting the traditional workplace and with so few of them (25%) signaling an intention to retire, we are about to witness one of the most profound periods of entrepreneurialism that our country has ever seen. The creation of this new income by older people will continue to accelerate the skew of wealth to the north of the age cohort (18 to 49) that has typically defined traditional marketing practice. If the power of marketing is about the consumer's power to purchase, it's time to start thinking about a shift in focus.

Part Two expands on the *Getting Better With Age* metaphor by learning more about *things* that get better with age. We'll look at classics like wine and cheese, and less obvious items like leather, cast-iron skillets, and even memories. While each of these things has technical or physical properties that help them improve with age, we will discover that these are of less importance relative to societal, social, and personal mores and context that influence how quality is perceived and thus defined. Is old wine actually better than young wine? The wine trade and its pricing model have us convinced of that, just as aging people have convinced themselves that it's better to be older than it is to be young. The relationship between things that get old and *people* who get old is fascinating and will help us tease out some really compelling analogies with clear implications.

Finally, Part Three – *50 Ways to Get Better With Age* – offers an abundance of simple, practical advice to help you create marketing campaigns that reflect a better understanding of the nuances that are critical in marketing to age. These insights reflect the real-world experiences of the author and the in-market successes of BoomAgers, the pioneering agency for aging founded by the author. Their potency lies in their simplicity and many are surprising in their obviousness. They are anecdotal and written in a light, entertaining manner to ensure that they are enjoyed and remembered.

There's an old adage that says: "All roads of life move toward the future." As marketers, it feels like we are at the proverbial fork in the road, and our future most certainly has a lot to do with the lives of aging consumers. If you intend to keep moving forward, the fork in the road forces a choice. We instinctively know that it's important to make choices in business, but we also know that making the right choice can be difficult. In avoiding the hard choices, we have to guard against the easiest way to fail, which is to make no choice at all. Wouldn't it all be much easier if we had a road map? Read on.

PART
ONE

Aged to Perfection

STILL BUBBLY

Deep within a Finland-controlled archipelago of some 6,500 small islands in the Baltic Sea, divers discovered a sunken schooner dating back to the second quarter of the 19th century. Within the hold of the ship, they found a voluminous amount of cargo, but one set of crates caught their eye. Realizing they found a wreck of immense worth, 168 bottles of 200-year-old champagne on the sea floor was a find worthy of celebration. They carefully raised the crates to the surface, but changing pressure caused some of the corks to pop off. The divers thought quickly and drank the centuries-old wine – which was surprisingly delicious and intact from seawater.

The divers brought the champagne to wine expert Ella Grussner Cromwell-Morgan whose assessment was as follows:

"Despite the fact that it was so amazingly old, there was a freshness to the wine. It wasn't debilitated in any way. Rather, it had a clear acidity which reinforced the sweetness. Finally, a very clear taste of having been stored in oak casks." [1]

It turns out, storing wine at the bottom of the Baltic Sea is actually a perfect place to age your wine, although, it's best to drink them earlier than a Schooner's hold would dictate.

---

[1] Vines, Richard. "World's Oldest Champagne Tastes Sweet After 200-Year Shipwreck." Bloomberg Business. http://www.bloomberg.com/news/articles/2010-11-17/world-s-oldest-champagne-survives-icy-shipwreck-surfaces-for-wine-tasting

CHAPTER
═══ ONE ═══
Living in the Age of Aging

We live in the Age of Aging, which means that more of us are living longer and "getting old" at an older age. This is life's way of offering a dividend, a bonus of extra years to extend our presence and influence on our personal world. This is great news if you're one of those people intent on extending your life so you can get to the bottom of your bucket list, but on a macro basis, aging is impacting the world in unprecedented and pervasive ways that must be reckoned with. Despite an abundance of global population statistics and the inevitability of mortality, the world has been slow to acknowledge that global aging is reshaping our cultural, political, and economic landscape in ways that are as irreversible as aging itself. It's as if we have our heads buried in the sands of time.

Some of the smartest minds in business and politics are choosing to be blind to global aging which, while vastly perplexing, can be logically explained in two ways. First, aging is fundamentally an unpleasant topic as it's associated with mortality, and it's human nature to abhor that which is unfavorable (death) and to embrace that which is favorable (life). Second, aging is about change, in the sense that it is a dynamic of life but also from the standpoint that *doing something* about global aging will require *changing something*.

There's a tendency to want to believe that change is glacial, that it takes place slowly over an extended period of time, virtually imperceptible to the naked eye. If so, it doesn't really capture our attention or command our action in any meaningful way. Even though change is a variable, we prefer to treat it as a constant. The notion of constancy satisfies our innate desire for the world to be orderly and predictable, and instead of addressing change, we reason that it will be someone else's job to deal with any unpredictable consequences long after we have moved on to a safe harbor.

The Global Coalition on Aging is one of the world's most prominent advocates for reshaping the way global leaders prepare for the 21st century's profound shifts in population aging. Through their focus on research, public policy analysis, advocacy, and communication, they are working to create innovative solutions to ensure that an aging world is productive as well as fiscally and politically sustainable.

One of the key areas of public policy debate is the need for constructive reform around a core issue: the ability of societies to provide an acceptable standard of living for their aging populations without burdening their young. Philosophically, there are two basic solutions to this dilemma: promote more elderly participation in the labor force or increase state-funded pension savings. While each of these is an obvious answer, both are currently impractical in many economies. When push comes to shove, addressing the old-age dependency burden may require a wholesale rethinking of retirement provision and the intertwined responsibilities of the personal, private, and public sectors.

The good news is that while global aging barely registered as a policy issue ten years ago, it has now at least become a topic of growing concern. The bad news is that despite all that entities like the Global Coalition on Aging are doing to promote positive change, global aging preparedness remains low. The world has yet to see a magnitude of progressive public policy shifts and social and cultural reform that corresponds with the significant impact that aging is going to have on human affairs.

This is because global aging is a glacier. While it is one of the largest moving things on earth, no one can see far enough beneath its surface to witness the powerful force that is at work. This force is transforming the landscape of our lives and reducing rock-solid tenets of the status quo into remnants of dust. While global aging is neither a force that we can stop nor reverse, we can do a much better job of understanding it and positively managing its impact. As some of the world's top business leaders, we have an obligation to do so, but just as importantly, it's smart business to do so.

Global aging has been underway for sometime. If you lived during the Roman Empire, you would have been lucky if you eked out 25 years of life.[1] By contrast, if we flash forward to the 20th century, we see that most of the world experienced a dramatic improvement in life expectancy. In some of the world's more developed and wealthier countries, we started the century with an expectation to live until we were 50, but by the end of the century, life expectancy had been extended to 75.

According to UN statistics for the period of 2005-2010, Japan has the world's highest life expectancy (82.6 years), followed by Hong Kong and Iceland at 82.2 and 81.8 respectively.[2] To paraphrase Mark Twain, when I get old I'm going to Japan because everyone gets older later there.

If we've been able to add 25 years to life expectancy in the last 100 years, what does the future hold, and at what point do we approach an upper limit?

While many aging experts believe that an upper limit exists, the escalation of life expectancy shows no evidence of slowing down. Between the years 1840 and 2007, average life expectancy progressed at the rate of approximately three months for each year of life.[3] But what's really noteworthy is the increasing life expectancy among members of the older population groups. The "oldest of the old" – people

85+ – are now 8% of the overall 65+ segment. This group is projected to grow 351% between today and 2050, compared with an increase of 188% in the 65+ segment and a 22% increase for adults under 65.[4]

While the "oldest old" are not the focus of this book, these statistics paint a dramatic picture of the future of global aging. To wit, there are currently more than 60,000 centenarians in the US and their numbers are projected to grow to 1,000,000 by 2050.[5] On a global basis, the number of centenarians in the world is projected to grow tenfold by 2050. Researchers have estimated that over the course of human history, the odds of attaining the age of 100 may once have been as high as one in 20,000,000 and may now be as low as 1 in 50 in low-mortality countries like Japan.[6] While scientists believe that humans are only capable of living to 120 (Mme. Jeanne Calment of France was 122 years old when she passed in 1997), the rate at which we are aging is challenging this long-held notion.[7]

If the world is aging because we're living longer, what's influencing longevity? While there are many theories, most agree that the major drivers of longevity are improved nutrition, health, and hygiene. While one could devote entire books to each of these topics, the key takeaway is that humans are benefiting from improvements in the quality of food, advances in medical science in the areas of both prevention and cure, and clean living habits that are curbing the spread of parasitic and infectious diseases. What's more, while we are benefitting from improvements to our world, we're also getting better about avoiding what's harmful in our world, e.g. tobacco, sun, pollutants, isolation, and more. Finally, the world's population is also benefitting from the improved availability of health-specific knowledge. Thanks to the expanded distribution of media and the creation of the internet, accessibility to knowledge has empowered people to proactively manage their wellness with less need for medical intervention.

While all of these conditions have contributed to the extension of our lives, none has had a more profound effect than improvements in medical science, particularly the science of aging. For many years, the primary focus of aging science was the treatment of *diseases* associated with aging, such as heart disease, neurological disorders, macular degeneration, and osteoporosis.[8] Now the focus is shifting to the factors that *influence* aging, particularly genetics. Researchers in this space believe that the duration of our lives may rely on the presence of a specific type of gene – categorized as a "longevity assurance" gene – which only some of us inherit.[9] This is best understood simply: long-lived parents have long-lived children. Scientists have revealed that the siblings of centenarians are four times more likely to live to the age of 90 versus those who are children of parents with average life expectancy; as for living to the same age as their centenarian parent, the likelihood is seventeen times greater for men versus eight for women.[10]

Just as the science of aging has traditionally focused on the negative side of aging (eg. disease) so too has medical research related to the brain. Now the focus on age-related neurological disorders (eg. Alzheimer's) is being balanced with emerging science regarding "successful brain aging".[11] Here again, we are beginning to learn that other long-held preconceptions of aging simply aren't true. As we age, our brains are in a constant state of reorganization, adapting to new events and experiences. In this regard, the aged brain is much more flexible in its ability to adapt to physical and psychological aspects related to our environment than we give it credit for.[12] Further, our mental lives improve in correlation to our physical, social, and intellectual activity (don't retire too quickly) while the language systems of the brain are tremendously resilient to age and remain vibrant throughout most of our lives.

Regardless of the branch of science, all of the reoriented focus on aging is dedicated to a common goal: to better understand the dynamics of aging so we can help people function at their best and they can experience a high quality of life across an extended lifetime. This is science dedicated to an understanding of the individual human condition so as to inform the creation of programs that broadly support human welfare.

Some years back, an intrepid explorer set out to find something that had eluded mankind since the beginning of time. His quest was not folly, as it had been years in the planning and had received funding from the highest levels of government. His team was top notch, his equipment was state of the art, and there was a genuine sense that he would succeed where others before him had failed. Ponce de Léon never did find the Fountain of Youth, which is not remarkable. What is remarkable is that a highly organized, government-funded endeavor showed that discovering eternal youth was not only a worthy pursuit, but also one with a more-than-likely chance of success.

History has clouded many of the details of this foray such that we may never know what it was that de Léon was *actually* seeking. What kind of youth did he expect to find? Would the fountain's waters turn back time to the days of one's youth? Lock you in time at the prime of your life? Was he seeking longevity instead of youth? Would the fountain's waters offer the promise of eternal life, and at what age? Would one really want to live forever? While these are all questions of youth, they are fundamentally the same questions that get at the answers we need to fully understand aging. Chances are you're not reading this book because you're a scientist. You're likely a person who is in a position to benefit in some way by better understanding what aging is and how to improve the lives of people who are aging. If so, the only relevant definition of youth or age is what the people living it feel it is.

So let's not call it healthy aging, normal aging, or successful aging. From my experience as someone dedicated to marketing to people of age – the people living in old age – most of them define aging as living. End states like mortality or morbidity are part of the bias that young people bring to aging, but these are not even remotely part of the active consciousness of Baby Boomers. On this point I must be very clear. When we talk about getting better with marketing to age, we are mostly referring to the Baby Boomers, a generation of US consumers born between the years of 1946 and 1964 which, at the time of this book's publication, range from 51 to 69 years of age. They are 76 million strong, they control 70% of the country's disposable income, and will soon represent 50% of the US adult population. They are the mass in mass marketing, and their years of consumerism have more than qualified them for the noteworthy title of Marketing's Most Valuable Generation.™

We make this distinction because there is a bias to think of age as a vast numerical span that spreads to the north of what a young person might define as a desirable age. In the conventional marketing practice that defines cohorts by age, the Boomers fall into the dreaded 50+ moniker, a catchall home for the castoffs whose status as a coveted 18- to 49-year-old consumer has expired. Sarcasm aside, it is important to make the distinction between the Boomers in the 50+ cohort and the generation that preceded them – the Silent Generation – as most marketers still believe that a younger consumer is more valuable than an older consumer. When viewed as the youngest generational sub-segment of 50+, there should be no question that the Boomers are, and will continue to be, a highly desirable target audience.

The Boomers live in the Age of Aging and they are defining aging as living. Most are striving to stay as great as they feel, and many are endeavoring to get even better. They're ignoring the stigma that one's numerical age defines who they are, and they're actively redefining all aspects of life as they live the age that they're feeling. In a world where aging is associated with dying, the Boomers are more alive than ever before.

It's as if they're living the words of poet Elizabeth Coatsworth who once said: "When I dream, I am ageless." The Boomers have always been ambitious dreamers, and more often than not, they have achieved that which they have conceived. As their lives have proceeded, their dreams have become ever more vivid, almost as if they are daring themselves to prove they still have what it takes to be great. Dreams? Perhaps, but they sure do seem pretty real. This generation is just getting started with the next act in their lives and it's going to be a fascinating show. Their dreams are real.

CHAPTER
═══ TWO ═══

We Have Become Them

It was a lifetime in coming, but it finally happened. In 2014, the last members of the largest and most influential generation in history turned 50 and crossed over to the "other side". For years, it had been common to think of someone of 50 years or more as being "old", that undesirable description of one who has proverbially gone "over the hill" in the direction of what lies on the other side. The hill had always been there, hiding in plain sight. The Baby Boomers just went about their daily business, pretending it was not there, almost as if aging was something that happened to everyone else but not them. Denial was okay because it worked. Anything was better than accepting that old age was inevitable and now frighteningly imminent.

The Baby Boomers were born into incredibly unique circumstances. After four dread-filled years of conflict, the explosions of World War II gave way to peace and a different kind of explosion – a global population boom. As the uncertainty of war faded, plans for the future grew brighter and families grew bigger. The American spirit had shown itself to be as irrepressible as ever. We had defeated a sinister enemy and shown the world our resolve, protecting the great American way of life. We had a sense that we could do anything and our country was brimming with optimism.

With this as their backdrop, the Baby Boomers came of age bathed in peace, prosperity, and the unrestricted freedom to express themselves and make their own choices. As the world grew up around them and in response to them, they began to get the sense that they were able to say and do what they wanted with a high likelihood that they would be listened to. Not only was the post-war society being shaped by post-war prosperity, it was also shaped by the demands and will of the Baby Boomers. While previous generations had been taught to be accepting of the circumstances that they inherited, the Boomers soon realized that they were empowered to change them.

Half a century later, the Boomers have inherited a new set of circumstances. The very generation that had perpetuated the stigma of age when they themselves were young is now on the receiving end of society's deeply entrenched stereotypes of age. The realization is setting in. By the very definition of age that they themselves had created, the Baby Boomers are now officially old and they don't like their new suit of clothes one bit.

Whether they are doing so consciously or subconsciously, the aging Baby Boomers are actively redefining aging. Aging, as we once knew it, is done. It is in the midst of a full makeover from something that was once universally seen as a blemish on life to a highlight that is now glorified as a positive. Aging is the new big thing and it's a good thing. If you believe in the Boomers' take on it, aging is well worth waiting a lifetime for.

This positive redefinition of aging has the notion of continuous improvement at its core. In our younger years, we were prone to believe that our lives would have three distinct phases: youth, middle age, and old age. Youth was the apogee of life, after which one descended into middle age (is there anything exciting about being in the middle?) and ultimately into the dark abyss that was seen as old age. This picture of life matches the image of the hill that we spoke of at the beginning of this chapter – life is essentially a journey to a summit followed by an uninspiring descent down the unseen back side.

After years of climbing through life, the Boomers eventually reached their originally conceived summit of life (think age 50) and, not surprisingly, they didn't like the view. So, they chose to declare it a false summit, and continued their climb, still rising in life toward a more glorious peak. Instead of life having three distinct phases, they were now experiencing it as one continuous, never-ending ascent. The Boomers truly believe that they are ageless and they've even convinced themselves that they are destined to get better every year. Onward they climb, with their view continuing to improve as they reach still new altitudes of life.

While the hill metaphor is an apt one, when stripped away it reveals a generation that is guilty of a blatant double standard – it was okay for the Boomers to malign old age when they were young, but now that the tables have been turned on them, they've decided to change the rules. While guilty as charged, they do have an alibi, and it holds up. The fact of the matter is that when the first of the Boomers came to life in 1946, average life expectancy was 64 years old. Seventy-eight million children grew up believing that the prime of their life would be sometime in their forties, but as they proceeded toward that prime, they gained the dividend of extra life, courtesy of the improvements in longevity. The 64-year-olds today are expected to live until they are 80. The view had changed and they liked what they saw.

The redefinitions don't end with age itself, as the Boomers are also redefining the things associated with aging. Remember that quaint concept known as retirement? Whether out of necessity or choice, a significant 41% of Boomers have indicated that they have no intention of leaving the office and going home for good.[13] Retirement today is all over the map. It's literally a blur of on again, off again and back on again behavior, as Boomers confront the realities and consequences of aging in the traditional workplace.

If loyalty and long-term employment are gone, so too is the image of a rocking chair, once a symbol of well-earned rest and relaxation after a long life of hard work. The image is gone because it's been reframed by reality, but also by the Boomers' new definition of aging. Aging is no longer about a sedentary life, no matter how enjoyable that actually might be. Instead, retirement is seen as a temporary pause before the transition to life's next income-generating performance. Retirement has been redefined as something they no longer want because they've realized they can't get it.

The end of life – to the extent that Boomers actually believe there is one – has also been redefined. Sixty-three per cent of Boomers have indicated their preference to age in place, to live their final years in the comfort of their own homes, providing for their own needs.[14] Gone is the image of blue-haired seniors filed away in nursing homes eating three square meals of soft food each day. Whether it's a reasonable expectation or not is not up for debate. The image of waiting for mortality in a home that is not yours is simply too unpleasant to fathom. Instead, it's been replaced with an acceptable scenario of living one's final years in a comfortable home equipped with life-simplifying technology and medical support offered by opportunistic industries only too happy to enable a massive generation's fantasy of aging in place.

While it's true that we have aged just as the Silent Generation did, that's the end of any similarity. Over the course of time, we have watched every new generation impact our world in ways that we could not have anticipated. We're doing it again now as we seek to understand the "Mysterious Millennials", a coveted new generation that continues to vex marketers with their enigmatic tendencies. The reason that we continue to be perplexed by new behaviors and attitudes is that we are making judgments based on the norms of past behavior. As my good friend and chairman of DigitasLBi and Razorfish – Rishad Tobaccowala – so eloquently says: "You can't put the future in the containers of the past."

Nothing that the Boomers have done or will do should surprise us if we approach them with an open mind. Our job as marketers is not to judge, but rather to seek to understand, and we must remember that what we learn today is probably going to change again tomorrow. While our journey to get better with age is going to reveal many surprises, at least we will know that one thing will remain obvious: it's time to dispense with the old thinking about getting old.

CHAPTER
THREE

Aging Is the Future of Living

So far, we've established that the world is aging and that we're living longer lives in unprecedented ways. Just as longevity has been numerically redefined, we're also psychologically redefining the dynamic of aging. Aging is now a positive thing – it's an advantage earned over a lifetime. Buoyed by this new orientation, people of age are bringing an optimistic perspective to life and approaching new endeavors with a level of vigor and vitality once associated only with youth.

If the aging consumer's outlook on life is changing, then we need to change the way we think of age; we will need a new definition to help us bring new meaning to what we are seeing. However, since most definitions are static, and aging is proving to be ever so dynamic, we will need a definition that illuminates what aging is today and also provides insight going forward.

Before we do so, let's bring some basic clarity to what aging is by confirming what it *is not*. First and foremost, it's not a number. Numbers are symbols used to express quantity, but the Baby Boomer consumers are looking at aging as quality – the enhanced quality of life that has come from a lifetime of experience *plus* the expectation of a sustained quality of life in the future. In this regard, aging is a spirit, it's a positive state of mind, and it's anything except a statistic.

It used to be that if you asked older people their age, they would avoid answering out of a fear of being stigmatized by their honesty. If you ask them today, you probably still won't get an answer but the reason will be different. They won't reveal their number because they don't believe that their true age is a true reflection of the age they *feel*. The aging consumer is telling us that feelings matter more than facts.

Next, aging is not about biology, it's about psychology. Granted, advances in medical science have improved our physical health and extended our life expectancy, but the science we're interested in is behavioral science. As marketers, we need to be able to understand why consumers think and act the way they do so we can tailor our offerings to their true needs; we also want to be better at predicting their future behavior. For these reasons, we will focus less on the physical consequences of aging in exchange for an improved understanding of the aging mind-set and how it affects their emotions and attitudes toward our products and services.

As for what aging is, I get asked that question often when I'm on the speaking circuit, and it's my chance to have a little fun with the topic. I'll often reply by saying that aging is: "When you no longer recognize the people in *People* magazine." Or even better: "Aging is when you choose your cereal for the fiber and not the prize." It's always interesting to watch the audience's reaction. The Millennials (1977-1995) and Gen Xers (1965-1976) laugh out loud, while the Boomers just smile and give me that knowing nod.

The very best definition of aging comes to us compliments of Joe Coughlin of MIT's Age Lab. The Age Lab is a multidisciplinary research program based in MIT's School of Engineering and has been at the forefront of aging solutions since 1999. They work with business, government, and NGOs to invent new ideas and translate technology into practical solutions that improve the quality of life for older people and their caregivers.[15]

When polled about the prospects of aging that worry them most, the majority of older people express concern over a potential loss in independence or mobility, as well as worries about social isolation. If you look more closely at an opportunity like mobility, you can appreciate what creative minds and industry can do if they team up on aging. As you can imagine, I spend a lot of time flying and I get to see a lot of what is going on inside airplanes. The next time you fly, count the number of passengers requiring wheelchair assistance in boarding. It is wonderful to see how much more efficient the airlines have become in easing the boarding and deplaning process for people with compromised mobility. Interestingly, that is also where the innovation ends.

While the carriers have improved at managing mobility – essentially to speed up the boarding and deplaning process to improve on-time performance – neither they nor the airplane manufacturers have done much to improve the in-flight experience for people of age. In today's age of counter-level appliances, is there a reason that heavy luggage is still hoisted to be stored overhead? And what about those miniature lavatories where even a fully mobile person has difficulty moving in such cramped quarters? We use the airline mobility example to highlight that there's not only a need to improve the quality of life for people in need, but there's also a significant business opportunity for carriers and manufacturers to deliver an improved, differentiated offering that generates increased consumer interest and improved fares. There are flatbed seats in international business class because innovation drove demand from the airlines' most valuable fliers: business travellers. Now think of what's possible if you're the first carrier to have an innovated experience for The Most Valuable Generation™ of consumers?

MIT's Age Lab's definition of aging is "the future of living". Earlier in the book, we set the tone by defining aging as living. This was the beginning of our deliberate effort to offset the bias that aging is about mortality. But the term living is not just about living in the moment, it is also reflective of the optimistic view that Boomers have of the years ahead. They are enthusiastically looking forward to what's next, which they see as a continuation of the life that they are enjoying today. And they want more – more years and more of the quality of life that they see as their norm. By defining aging as the future of living, we capture the dynamic aspects of aging and we're in lock step with the Boomers' psychology of aging as they joyously move toward the future.

The future that they aspire to is one of uncompromised living. In light of the improvements in healthcare, nutrition, and avoidance, they're living longer and stretching the definition of what they see as their prime years. They aspire to – if not expect – a life that will not be limited by the traditional symptoms of age. I wouldn't want to be in the cane business these days with what's happening in the hip replacement business. Many of my friends have already had their second hip done and are good to go for another 20 years of full-on physical activity. What's more, the *New York Times* even reported that some women are electing to have hip surgery to improve flexibility and sexual pleasure.[16] Hey, if it feels good, do it.

The uncompromised living that the Boomers want is characterized by a focus on wellbeing, joy, and growth. While each of these aspects of living can meaningfully improve the quality of life, given that they are so inter-related, a considered approach to life also has the ability to enhance one's lifestyle in exponential ways.

Wellbeing is the foundation of the quality of life. When it comes to aging consumers, the wellbeing that they're seeking goes beyond the typical interpretation of this term – physical health. While they may bring a healthy dose of denial to their outlook on personal health, they're also realistic. They know that aging will eventually take things away from them without asking permission, but they don't seem to be terribly fixated on that eventuality. Partially because they're living in the moment, but also because their instincts are telling them that they can rely on their ability to persevere, as they have for a lifetime. They have racked up extensive experience in overcoming adversity and they've demonstrated to themselves that they possess the will to triumph over anything that aging throws their way.

Wellbeing is also about emotional and spiritual contentedness. When we talk about someone who has "come to grips with reality", we are speaking about their ability to put things in their proper perspective. They have interpreted their experiences or reality in a way that brings meaning to them, and with meaning comes understanding, order, and ultimately a restoration of control. Imagine the importance of having this degree of personal contentedness as you take on the unpredictable challenges of aging. It is an essential ingredient to prepare you for an uncompromised life and to defend it once aging starts hurling compromises your way.

As they look to enjoy uncompromised living while knowing that much is out of their ultimate control, they've adopted a practical outlook – they are striving not for perfection, but for delight. They know that they are capable of being the masters of their own delight if they focus on joy and growth.

Many people are surprised when I say there's joy in aging. The response is usually incredulous. How could there possibly be happiness in advancing age, morbidity, and the inevitability of mortality? Don't take it from me. There is scientific evidence that people get happier as they get older. While there are differing theories as to why this is, most agree that later-life contentedness is the combined result of accumulated wisdom and confidence, as well as a general acceptance of aging. Older people are at a stage in life where they can reflect on their positive life experiences and savor their accomplishments. The anxiety associated with striving is replaced by the satisfaction of a life well lived.

The notion of growth in aging – which is central to the subject of this book – represents Boomers at their defiant best, a radical generation that is once again determined to change the undesirable circumstances that they have inherited. They are defying the unrelenting progress of aging with a self-imposed commitment to continue to learn and grow. They see this phase of their life as just another act in a long-running production, with much more entertainment still ahead. At a time when the old definition of aging had them getting ready to stop, they're just getting started, and the virtues of life-long growth are as compelling as ever. Aptly, this is the generation that's not *getting* older; it's the one that's *growing* older.

For many Boomers, the most important aspect of the future of living is figuring out the future. We've already indicated that the majority of them have no intention of retiring, but it's not yet clear that the majority of them know what they want to be doing when they're not retiring. What is clear is that our optimistic tendencies have us idealizing what's next. Hey, if we're not going to be able to retire to our own private island, we might as well be enjoying our next job.

As a quintessential Boomer, I fall squarely into the above camp. I have little or no desire to stop working, but I do want to work differently, and I have an idealized image of what that looks like. After years of working in offices in the city, I want to work outdoors in the country. I also want to maximize the aspects of work that I enjoy most while minimizing those that I like least. My vision of "retirement" is to work as a rental property owner, caretaker, and marketer. If I were to have the financial wherewithal, I would buy a few fixer-uppers on Nantucket Island, one of my favorite destinations. Having grown up on a farm working jobs that required manual labor – and having spent the majority of my life in the service industry – I long for a chance to return to work that requires manual competency. My idealized vision of the future has me restoring these homes with my hands and my tools, and marketing them to vacationers who can enjoy the benefits of my craftwork. What a great thought that is – using my hands for something other than typing emails.

As the revered Chinese philosopher Confucius (551-479 BC) once said, "Choose a job that you love and you will never have to work another day in your life." If the Boomers truly believe that the future of living is going to get better, and that their future is going to include work, then clearly they will be aspiring to do work that they love. Given that there will be fewer and fewer traditional employment opportunities available to them and that appeal to them based on the above criteria, they will be looking to find passion in jobs that they can create for themselves, modelled in response to their personalized ideal of work. The generation that grew up empowered to make change is now in control of changing its very own futures. All roads are moving to the future, and so far, the Boomers are in the driver's seat.

If the Baby Boomer generation was to have its own advertising slogan, it would be something like, "Live longer and put more life into every day." You have to wonder if their favorite beer had it right all those years ago when Schlitz said, "Go for the gusto!" Well, they did and they still are. The future of living remains bright for the generation that continues to drink up round after round of life. Hey, pass me another. Does anyone know when last call is?

A SHELL OF ITS FORMER SELF

Horseshoe crabs are considered "living fossils." The earliest horseshoe crabs are dated back to the Ordovician period that lasted almost 45 million years, beginning 488.3 million years ago. Rightly so, looking at a horseshoe crab on the eastern beaches of North America, you immediately flash back in time and realize you are witnessing a creature that is one of the oldest organisms still on this earth.

Protected by a hard shell and long spiny tail, the horseshoe crab is built for longevity, by protecting all of its important body parts from modern pecking beasts such as sea gulls and osprey. Considered a delicacy in Southeast Asia, and mainly used for bait in North America, it's recently that the medical community has discovered that the horseshoe crab's blue blood has life-saving abilities. It seems when crabs are cut, their blood immediately froths around the laceration and fights off bacteria and any impending infection. When the blood is humanely extracted from the crabs and injected into a batch of human vaccines, it can indicate whether bacteria is present and if the vaccines are safe for distribution.

Who would think that one of the oldest living organisms on the planet would have these super protectionary functions – just one look at them would have you believing that everyone does.

CHAPTER
FOUR

Living in the Moment

J ust when you think you understand this generation, you realize you don't. They are a living paradox, and as they live longer we will bear witness to even more bewildering aspects of their behavior. At times, it seems as though the harder we work to comprehend the Baby Boomers, the more they surprise us with inexplicable conduct contradictory to the norms we thought were predictive of behavior. While the very premise of this book posits that the Baby Boomers are looking to the future of living with an optimistic outlook, there is a mountain of evidence that indicates they are also living in and for the moment. How is it that a generation that has embraced their longevity with a feeling of agelessness is simultaneously fixated on the short term? Perplexing indeed; they are living like there's no tomorrow, even though they're also determined to live life like it has no end.

For those of us in marketing who seek to understand consumer behavior today so we can predict the future, conundrums like this can be frustrating. We want to believe that life follows an orderly pattern, because order provides the constancy that in turn promotes predictability. However, the behavior that the Boomers are displaying as they live in the Age of Aging is anything but constant. This is because aging is not a static event in time, like most other consumer behavior that we study. Instead, it's a dynamic, and as such is subject to a different kind of constancy – the constancy of change.

If aging is about constancy of change, then the aging consumer is naturally going to be prone to act randomly. As predictable as it is that tomorrow brings a new day, it is equally as unpredictable as to what that new day will bring. While we would like to think that we can plan – and we do – in the end the natural order of things is in control (new events occur each new day). We are the ones who are "out of control" – we're acting randomly in reaction to the new events of each new day. We're all making it up as we go because we've never been where we are now.

We have defined aging as the future of living, but it's also true that the plan for the future begins today. After all, today is the only day we can control in light of the fact that yesterday is gone and tomorrow has yet to come. Viewed in this context, aging is a series of todays; one's outlook for a long life well lived thus becomes a vision of numerous todays lived to their fullest potential. Albert Einstein characteristically summed this up brilliantly: "Life is a preparation for the future; and the best preparation for the future is to live as if there were none."[17]

Since my work requires spending most days with other Baby Boomers, I'm always on the lookout for anecdotal evidence of our philosophies on aging. When I ask other Boomers what years they believe to be the best of their lives, the answer is almost always the same: "Right here, right now." A recent poll by Harris Interactive (a widely respected provider of public opinion survey data in the US for more than 40 years) asked a representative sample of Americans of all generations to define the perfect age, and the answer was 50; ten years prior, the response was 41.[18] This is only surprising if you are not a student of aging. This survey response is yet more evidence of what happens when a big chunk of the population ages and changes their mind along the way. When you live in the now, the age you are right now is bound to be perfect.

Just as we can't control yesterday or tomorrow, most aging people lament that they can't control the speed with which life is passing; it often prompts the question of why time seems to go by faster as we get older. My father used to always complain that there weren't enough hours in the day to get everything done and I can still remember my youthful disregard for those words of wisdom (if I only knew then what I know now). Growing up in the '60s and '70s, schools would empty each summer to the sounds of Alice Cooper's popular song, *School's Out* and our lazy carefree days of summer felt like weeks, almost as if we were living our own version of Hollywood's Endless Summer. Now summer feels like a rushed span of four weeks between Memorial Day and Labor Day, remembered more for the things we regret not doing than the things we did.

There are many reasons why life seems to accelerate as we age, the most popular being mathematical – the more days you have lived, the less each new day represents as a percentage of your total life. While this is certainly a plausible explanation, at the end of the day we lack a scientific explanation for the acceleration of life, as we just don't know enough about how humans assess time, given that there is no one area of the brain dedicated to time perception.[19] Since it's becoming ever more obvious that life is accelerating and that we can do little to slow it down, we're responding in the only way we know how: we're putting more into every day to get more out of life.

It's fascinating to see how this compensatory behavior plays out in my own life, particularly when I'm vacationing. There was a time when I viewed vacation as my opportunity to enjoy pleasantries denied to me by the rigors of the workweek. As such, it was not uncommon to find me relaxing on a beach, idly soaking up the sun for hours, entertained only by some great beach reads. A day enjoyed that way was almost always capped off with a nap prior to dinner, followed by an early bedtime. These many years later I look back on those "hedonistic" times with a mixture of envy and angst; envy because I realize that I am no longer wired to derive pleasure from inactivity, and angst because I regret that I didn't spend my precious free time more wisely. You can probably see where this is going. Today, my vacations are packed with endless, exciting activities fuelled by a new philosophy that comes only with age – I have to make the most out of every moment because every moment matters now more than ever.

The other way aging consumers tend to compensate for time lost to the speed of life is to *make* new time. While we obviously don't have the ability to create incremental time in the day, we have convinced ourselves that we can make more time for the things that matter by decreasing time spent on activities from which we derive less utility. In other words, we are making more time by making the time we have more productive. It's easier for an aging consumer to make choices like this because they have benefit of a lifetime of experiences to help them decipher between those activities that are valuable to them versus those that are not. After years of saying yes to everything and everyone – especially in our roles as parents and employees – we're now more empowered to make time management choices on our own behalf. We're learning that "no" can be a very powerful word, not only as an expression of control ("It's my life, I can decide") but also for its liberating effect ("Look what I'm free to do now").

Aging consumers are also bringing more determination to their considerations. While it was once acceptable to muse and mull ambitions both small and large – often with nothing coming from such grand thought – Boomers are now much more intent to do the things that they talk about doing. Colloquialisms like "We should really do dinner some time" or "We should really go on that trip" are giving way to concrete planning, commitment, and action. The attitude seems to be, "Let's stop talking about it and let's do it." After all, there's no time like the present.

If you're an aging consumer, living in the now is a strategy that works. It helps you feel vital and productive in a life that gets better by the day – better with age. If you can only live your life one day at a time, this sure feels like the right approach. On the flip side, it's also possible that this short-term orientation to life may have more compromising implications in the long run.

At the top of this list is the worry that the Boomers have not saved properly for their future, and given that they are expected to live longer, there's a reasonable risk that they will outlive their resources. According to a recent Boston College study, more than one in two Americans are at risk of being unable to maintain their preretirement standard of living once they retire, up from 30% in 1989.[20] A study by the Employee Benefit Research Institute in May 2012 found that 44% of aging Americans might not have enough money to meet even their basic needs in retirement.[21]

Years ago, loyal employees could count on pension plans to make up the difference between personal savings and retirement living expenses. Now only 26% of all workers have some type of pension plan, while 58% do not participate in any type of employer-based retirement plan.[22]

Putting aside what money they may or may not have saved for the future, Boomers are also facing some significant cost-of-living pressures in the here and now. Many of them are providing for their parents and their adult children at a time when they are bumping up against employment-generated income limitations for the first time in their working lives.

It's estimated that one in eight Americans between the ages of 40 and 60 is simultaneously supporting themselves, aging parents, and grown children, and the outlook is not positive. Forty per cent of Boomers expect their adult children to move back in (at the moment, 13% of adult children actually do) while 30% expect their parents to move in too.[23]

What's more, the Boomers are reaching retirement age and exiting the traditional workplace at the rate of 10,000 a day for the next 17 years. In light of their savings history and current cost-of-living pressures, this is not the time to curtail a reliable stream of income. The need for sustained income explains why some 65% of Boomers plan to work past age 65 or do not plan to retire at all.[24] Many will need to find or create employment opportunities to service their on-going if not permanent cash flow needs.

There was once a traditional plan for aging, wherein retirees prepared for their non-income-generating years by preserving the value of their greatest asset: the large homes in which they raised their families. Before the advent of interest-only or variable-rate mortgages, most homeowners locked into a fixed-rate mortgage payment that grew easier to pay as one's earning potential improved over time. Given that most of these conventional mortgages had 30-year terms – a period roughly equivalent to the time it took to get the last of the children through college and out of the house – a responsible homebuyer actually ended up becoming a home owner, fully in possession of a significant asset that could be liquidated for retirement income.

Putting aside the impact that nonconventional mortgages have had on the Boomers' ability to increase equity in their homes, what's more alarming is the dilutive growth in home equity loans and reverse mortgages. *Inside Mortgage*, a housing industry trade publication, revealed that homeowners over the age of 62 took out $15.3 billion in reverse-mortgage loans in 2013, an increase of over 20% versus the prior year. While the reverse mortgage instrument was created to help homeowners manage dire financial circumstances, they are increasingly being used to meet ordinary living expenses, which is a very concerning trend. While there is certainly nothing traditional about this generation, it's pretty clear that the traditional model for funding retirement is no longer an option for most Baby Boomers.

While it's hard to discount these facts, we must never underestimate the resourcefulness and resolve of this unprecedented generation. Their optimism and will to influence their circumstances is profound, and we can only wait to see what's really going to happen. It doesn't much matter that traditional jobs will disappear for people of age, as all indications are that they will create new ones for themselves, facilitated by the ease and omnipresence of enterprise-enabling technology; where there's a will to make money, there's never been a better way.

What's more, thanks to the generational frugality of their parents, many of the Boomers will also benefit from an aggregate inheritance estimated to be worth almost twenty trillion dollars over the next 20 years.

If the Boomers' penchant for living in the now feels a bit like a generational *carpe diem*, then consider what the Roman poet Horace intended when he originally wrote those words as part of a longer phrase: "Carpe diem, quam minimum credula postero." Translated, this means "Seize the day, put very little trust in tomorrow."[25] As has been this generation's modus operandi for their entire lives, here again we see that they want it all and are doing all that they can to make it happen. By viewing aging as the future of living they are bringing specificity and positivity to a future that is uncertain and prone to be unpleasant. By living in the now, they are hedging their bets on the future. They're proactively contending with the possibility of a "what if?" scenario by embracing a "what now?" lifestyle, leaving little to chance for a future that they can control by living large today. This generation has shown no intention of slowing down, yet alone stopping, and is living life on fast forward. They're not just moving at the speed of life, they're setting a new speed limit for their age and going places that other generations never dreamed possible. There's a lot of road under their wheels, and miles more stretching out into the distance. Their epic journey continues for now, and while the destination remains unknown to all, we do know one thing for sure − their lives are getting more interesting by the day.

CHAPTER
FIVE

™ Fueling the Longevity Economy

ging is an economic stimulus package. Just think about the economic implications of adding decades to life expectancy each century. As people live longer and continue to contribute to the economy either as wage earners, taxpayers, or spenders, they are extending and expanding their national economies in proportion to their incremental years lived. Shortly after the turn of the 19th century, when a young British economist named John Maynard Keynes revolutionized economic thinking and the role of government stimulus, he scarcely could have imagined the impact that longevity alone would have in permanently transforming the world's economic landscape.

We live in the Age of Aging, an undeniably potent force that is permeating virtually every aspect of our lives while reshaping our economic context. Oxford Economics refers to this as the Longevity Economy, the sum total of economic activity associated with people over the age of 50.[26] Putting aside the implications of this economy for a moment, let's merely ponder its existence. In 1900, global life expectancy was only about 34 years. It would take another 50 years before life expectancy reached 50. Coming out of World War II (WWII) when the first Baby Boomers were born, we were a one-economy world. The economic value of being 50 or older did not even exist – in theory or in actuality – yet here we are today, largely as a consequence of the Baby Boom and longevity, discussing the benefits of an entirely new and *incremental* economy. If you're a government economist, this is like receiving a bonus you weren't expecting to get.

Oxford quantifies the longevity economy of the US as consisting of 106 million people who generate over seven trillion dollars of economic value per year, an amount that is expected to nearly double to 13.5 trillion dollars by 2032.[27] If you put this number in the context of our Gross Domestic Product (GDP), the longevity economy in the US today is larger than any other country's *total* economy, with the exception of the broader US economy and China, and by 2032, it will represent *more than half* of our country's GDP.[28] Let this sink in. If you're not interested in marketing to age, that's akin to saying that it's not worth doing business in any markets other than the US and China. Remember all of the fervor to set up businesses in the emerging BRIC (Brazil, Russia, India, and China) markets? The US longevity economy at $7.1 trillion is larger than that of Brazil, Russia, and India combined ($6.3 trillion). There was, and continues to be, more potential in marketing to age right here in our very own country than all that is at stake in the broader economies of the hottest foreign countries.

What's driving all this value? Fundamentally, two things: changing demographics and changing behavior within the new demographics. In the year 2000, the number of Americans over the age of 50 represented about 42% of the population of adults aged 25+, and by 2013, that number grew to 51%, and is expected to reach 54% by 2032.[29] As the distribution of our population continues to skew older, and those older people's economic propensities remain more or less unchanged, the sum total value of the 50+ economic activity is logically going to increase.

What's more revealing, however, is what the participants in the longevity economy are doing differently to trigger economic expansion. Let's start with aging itself. One has to ponder the existentialism of aging – as life expectancy and longevity increase, are we extending old age or are we expanding middle age? Since there's no right or wrong answer here, the only way we can answer this question is to identify the activities that used to be associated with middle age (eg. working, peak productivity) and then assess the extent to which these activities may be continuing longer and at an older age today.

For starters, middle age is generally defined as the period between young adulthood and the onset of "old" age, which is already problematic given that we've discovered that the alleged "old" people are actively redefining what it means to be old. Be that as it may, the ages corresponding to the middle-age life period are generally ages 40 to 60. This is the definition of middle age that persists from the Boomers' young age when their parents were in their years of peak productivity, raising a family and working for "the man". In this sense, middle age was seen as ending at the point that one's productivity began to yield diminishing returns. One simply retired, and at that point, they knowingly and willingly opened the door to old age.

Whether out of financial necessity or personal preference, more aging Americans are choosing to work longer than ever before. According to a survey conducted by Merrill Lynch in 2013, 71% of pre-retirees planned to continue some type of work as they passed retirement age (65); over half of the respondents indicated that they planned to start a new career in a paying position.[30] What's more, a 2011 MetLife Foundation/Civic Ventures study revealed that close to nine million Americans between the ages of 44 and 70 were in some type of encore career, with another 31 million claiming an interest in doing the same.[31]

The longevity economy's members represent approximately two thirds of all employment, which means two thirds of all wages paid in the US.[32] Since the government loves to tax our paychecks, Americans who are 50 and older represent nearly 50% of federal tax revenue.[33]

Sustained employment is the key behavior fueling the longevity economy. There is a fundamental difference in the economic impact of those who are retired (and dependent on fixed sources of income, including government-guaranteed benefits) compared with those who continue to earn new, taxable income well past typical "retirement" age. If the ability to work and remain productive define middle age, then we would seem to have our answer. Longevity is not extending old age, it's expanding middle age. If you're among those who are aging, you probably like this positive spin – more to come.

So if you're marketing to age, what are some of the implications of the longevity economy that need to be on your radar?

We've touched on the first and most important consequence (and driver) of the longevity economy: sustained employment. So much of the bias that society and businesses have toward aging is related to dated perceptions of retirement. We still tend to believe that an aging consumer is one who has by and large stopped working. Since so much of our life's identity and purpose tends to be defined by what we *do*, once we stop the "doing" part of our lives, it's assumed that the tide of life has turned and our importance and value has begun to ebb. This is why the myth persists that the younger consumer is more valuable than the older consumer.

One can perpetuate myths all that they want, but the US Department of Labor's statistics don't lie. More aging people are working longer, which means they are behaving like younger people longer – they have a reliable source of income that fuels spending and the continuation of middle age consumption patterns. There are two implications here. First, if you're marketing to 18- to 49-year-olds, you need to consider the fact that more 50+ people are acting like they *are* 18 to 49 than ever before, and second, 50+ consumers are not living on fixed income, mired in set ways. They are behaving like younger consumers. I repeat: age is not a number, and if you market by the numbers you will be missing out on a number of dollars. Yes, the aging consumer still consumes.

The next major implication of the 50+ economy is aging consumers' focus on the simplification and streamlining of virtually every aspect of their lives. If you consider that so much of our capitalistic adult lives is focused on career success and material gain, by the time one gets to be 50, they've probably accumulated lots of stuff. We're not talking about cleaning out the attic; instead, we're talking about the consequence of changes in values as people age and in reaction to age. Things that seemed important to own along the way take on a new hue and get the heave-ho to either make room for something more relevant for their new lifestyle, or simply to get by with less because less has a way of becoming more as one ages. Herein is another example of why "it takes one to know one". If you are young and aspiring to have a great family and a successful life, you are in acquisition mode. Once you've experienced the joy of acquiring what life can afford you, the new joy in life is to lighten your load, to eschew the quantity of material things in favor of more quality experiences. Why tow the boat all the way to the lake again when I can fly to Paris and float on the Seine? Unlike material things, experiences bring joy without maintenance.

If you're in the business of aging, "Aging in Place" is the place to be. This is the term that's being used to describe the aging generation's desire to spend their final years in the comfort of their own homes, enabled by advances in housing amenities and the on-premise administration of health services. This is not a whim – it's happening as we speak. According to the American Association of Retired Persons (AARP), some 90% of seniors say they want to live in their homes as they grow older, and even if they're guilty of not fully anticipating the implications of advanced age, that's still about a massive number of older folks who will be staying put.

The term "assisted living" was created as a more sensitive and politically correct substitute for "retirement home", and suggested that these were places you could go to continue to live, versus preparing to die. That's a convenient alibi if you're an adult child making a difficult choice of how to provide for an aging parent, but if you're a savvy senior in today's world, you're seeing right through the smoke. Boomers want to live where they've always lived and want assistance administered there, not at a "home" away from home. The burgeoning field of telemedicine has enabled people who are aging in place to transmit essential medical data to healthcare professionals who can monitor their condition remotely. It is also being used to track movement and other behaviors within the home to assure family members that all is well, and if not, to provide the opportunity for timely intervention.

Other progressive care providers and retailers are taking their products and services directly to the home rather than waiting for the customer to cross their bricks-and-mortar threshold. Smart folks like Walgreen's are delivering critical medications and fluids to customers' homes and administering them in the home by deploying visiting nurses. All of this innovation helps aging consumers enjoy uncompromised quality of life within the comfort of their own homes, while also not burdening local healthcare facilities with the need to service an increasing number of visits for the routine administration of medicines.

Finally, technology is a thread that's intertwined throughout the entire longevity experience, beginning with the ability to support telemedicine practices to its ability to enhance connectivity, mobility, and the simplification of daily lifestyles. Another common misperception is that aging people are intimidated by technology and use it only sparingly, mostly when they don't have an option. In actuality, the opposite is true – older adults seek it out as a means of validating their own desired self-image of being vital and connected in a modern world, as if to say, "Hey, if I have the latest iPhone, I'm clearly not falling behind the curve."

To the extent that technology has enabled social media, it has also helped the aging consumer stay connected with friends and family. To many people's surprise, they actually spend more time online than either Gen X or Gen Y (that's right, the Millennials) with most of that time devoted to the use of social networks to connect with friends and participate in social causes and advocacy.[34]

While the topic of this chapter has been the longevity economy, your focus needs to be on the longevity effect. Your biggest opportunities will come from understanding the *consequences* of such a significant number of wealthy people living longer and living more actively than their predecessors. The overarching consequence is that many are just now discovering that we're living in a very different world than we realize. We may think we live in a world of modern marketing, networked media, and digital solutions, but if you step back to see the big picture, that world of marketing lives in the broader ecosystem of the Age of Aging. If you embrace the longevity effect, you will aspire to improve marketing to age so you can capitalize on all of the uncontested potential inherent in this emerging market. If you choose to ignore it – for any of the historical reasons that marketers disdain the aging population – you risk sitting on the side-lines as smart money gets in the game of global aging. The best companies we know are those taking a long-term outlook and acting accordingly. If we also know that massive opportunity exists in targeting the aging economy, it stands to reason that the best companies' long-term strategies are going to include marketing to longevity. Growth can be elusive these days, but this is one opportunity that shouldn't get away from you.

A HUNGER FOR LIFE

Susannah Mushatt Jones, a resident of Brooklyn, New York, is a supercentenarian who at the age of 116 years, was recently named the world's oldest living person. When many of us hear of someone attaining this incredible feat, our first reaction is to wonder what attributed to his or her longevity. Others that are Ms. Jones' junior have cited daily constitutions such as three Miller High Life beers and a shot of whisky, or five push-ups, or even foot massages in olive oil.[2] But Susannah Jones credits her longevity to lots of sleep and a daily lumberjack breakfast consisting of grits, scrambled eggs and four strips of bacon! She also has a penchant for luxury lingerie and enjoys barbecue feasts with her family on occasion.[3]

While it's not as life affirming as 12 daily cigars or "staying away from men," Ms. Jones has earned the accomplishment of living the longest of all of us; we humans will never tire of wondering what habit or life decisions will keep us on this planet as long as possible.

---

[2] Waxman, Olivia B., "13 Secrets to Living Longer From the World's Oldest People." Time.com. http://time.com/3731504/longevity-secrets-worlds-oldest-person/

[3] Dunn, James. "World's Oldest Person, 115, is Brooklynite who eats four strips of bacon every morning and likes to wear 'fancy' lacy lingerie." Mailonline. http://www.linkza.net/daily/news/article-3131587/World-s-oldest-person-115-eats-four-strips-bacon-morning-likes-wear-fancy-lacy-lingerie.html

CHAPTER
SIX
The Old Rush is Underway

Few things are more motivating than the prospect of getting rich quickly. No matter our lot in life, most of us fantasize about striking it rich. Folly? Perhaps, but dreams have a way of sustaining us when reason fails. We can all thank Pandora for leaving hope in the box to help guide us to persevere when the going gets rough.

Business is a serious affair and we like to think that it's not a proper place for the silliness of dreams. Dreams lack discipline and anyone who knows a thing or two about business knows that success demands tangibles like vision, objectives, strategies, plans, and metrics. We apply process to our thinking to promote discipline and we prefer to think inside the box, where the presence of precedent gives us assurance of success. Thinking outside the box is encouraged but it's mostly rhetoric to appease the marketing culture's obligation to be creative. Dreams are the stuff of our imaginations and there's no place for them in businesses that value intelligence.

All of that said, we still dream in the workplace. Most of us are confronted with escalating expectations, to be delivered with fewer resources in less time, and in markets that are more competitive than ever before. We want to believe that there's an easier, faster way to deliver results, so we pretend to brainstorm about the possibilities (there's no such thing as a bad idea), when we're actually sharing our dreams. In today's ultra-demanding business environments, the dream is to do business where no one else is — to have a monopoly on a lucrative idea, to make a market where one does not currently exist.

This fast-growth scenario is also known as an emerging marketing strategy. Traditionally, business has defined an emerging market geographically, such that when the economic or political environment in a third-world country starts to look like a second-world opportunity, we uncoil like a spring to quickly establish a business presence on new soil. At some point, the world starts to run out of emerging markets, and if you're still looking to do business where no one else is, a map will not do you much good. However, if you free yourself from the definition of an emerging market as being geographical, a whole new world of opportunity opens up. Look no farther than global aging. The next big emerging market is not geographic, it's demographic — and it better be on your mental map.

In my first book I coined the phrase "The Old Rush" to refer to the sensational wealth available to those who move first on global aging. Inherent in the word "rush" is a strong element of mania —best defined as an addictive and excessive level of unreasonable enthusiasm. A high-octane version of this lured countless conservative folks to risk all for a chance at gold when its discovery at Sutter's Mill in Coloma, California, was announced in 1848. Word of the discovery spread quickly, and by the end of the following year, some 300,000+ prospectors (aka 49ers) had endured tremendous hardship to travel to California, not just from the United States but from every corner of the world.[35] Many recall the Gold Rush as a domestic phenomenon, just as they associate the Baby Boomer exclusively with America. In truth, the concept of the Old Rush is every bit as global as the original Gold Rush, but infinitely more valuable.

The aspect of the Old Rush that's most relevant to getting better with age is the need to move first — after all, there's a reason it's called the Old *Rush*. Anytime or anywhere there is an opportunity to grow quickly, success is going to favor those who have an opportunistic bias and are willing to take on the risk of acting first to secure the greatest riches. I like to refer to the prospectors of the 1849 Gold Rush as the original "first movers" – they literally stopped what they were doing and *moved* west to position themselves for success, to literally get *on* the gold. The ones who arrived first found nuggets on the ground; those who waited and followed when it was "safe" had to dig and pan for dust.

While it clearly required resourcefulness, perseverance, and optimism to succeed during the Gold Rush, imagine the courage it took to make the decision to go west in the first place. Of course, the prospect of finding gold was a very real incentive that emboldened many, but it's also important to consider some of the significant barriers that they faced in simply getting into the gold business. These included traveling to California, figuring out where the gold was once you got there, and then determining the best technique(s) for getting the gold out of the ground.

The least appreciated aspect of the Gold Rush was the ordeal that most of the prospectors went through just to get to the gold. The infrastructure that we take for granted today simply did not exist in 1849, and in the absence of continuous roads or rail lines, there were only three options for getting to the West Coast: two by sea and one by land. It took a special breed of entrepreneur to take the long voyage around Cape Horn, across the Panama Isthmus or more typically than not, 2,000 miles of rugged cross-country travel by land via rail, horse, wagon, and foot.

Once the fortunate prospectors got to California, the next stage of critical planning kicked in: staking a claim and sourcing the gear and provisions needed to extract the gold from the ground and sustain oneself in the wilderness for extended periods of time. This gearing-up process had all of the hallmarks of modern-day supply chain management, but without the help of inter-enterprise systems from providers like SAP.

If you consider this risk in the context of the Old Rush – marketing to age – it makes the barriers that most marketers believe they're facing seem downright trivial. Many brands are not moving toward the gold in marketing to age for some basic reasons. Some believe there's gold where they currently stand, and if they simply continue to do what they've always done, they'll be rewarded with the riches that will come from converting the next generation to their brand. Others know there's gold in marketing to age, but given that their organization lacks a precedent or best practice for marketing to age, they're hesitant to go where no one has been before, especially since the risk-reward posture of most organizations today does not encourage anything resembling risk.

When you study the events of the Gold Rush relative to the contemporary trade-offs associated with marketing to age, what's really remarkable is that the prospectors were willing to make a substantial sacrifice to get to the gold; they left something behind to be able to move forward. I like to refer to what they left behind as their metaphorical "east" as they sought to head west. The east for many of the miners was the comfort of home and an established, predictable way of life that provided a sustainable existence, but not much more. By contrast, the west meant gold, which meant transformative wealth. Many of those who went west envisioned that they would only do so for as long as it took to strike it rich, and then they would return home to their awaiting family and homestead to lead a more comfortable, secure existence.

To continue this metaphor, let's define the east as continuing to market to the 18- to 49-year-old cohort, and the west as breaking the unfamiliar ground of marketing to the aging consumer. Marketing to the 18- to 49-year-old consumer had led to so much success in the past, not because the numbers had some magic to them but because the 18-49 age group was populated by the largest generation in the history of marketing. With such success – and precedent – it's understandable that there was a certain amount of comfort associated with that target choice – comfort derived from *familiarity*.

By contrast, there was nothing familiar about the west, and just thinking about the prospects of succeeding there was anything but comfortable. At first blush, marketing to age is not an easy choice, but if you're willing to start by leaving some of the conventions of your current approach behind – in favor of a more innovative, more rewarding approach – you will find that your load will soon lighten and progress in a new direction will come more easily and readily.

While leaving familiarity behind feels risky, don't spend too long fretting about it. In truth, the core principles of marketing to 18- to 49-year-olds are mostly transferable to a 50+ model. *What* you need to do to create brand preference and loyalty with an aging consumer won't change all that much. The key difference between the two cohorts is in *how* you do it. Did the 49ers know much about *how* to prospect for gold before they left home? Not a stitch. Yet they weren't deterred because they were willing to rely on what they *did* know and trust that they would find the resourcefulness and creativity to figure out what they didn't know.

Hopefully all this talk of gold has you itching to get better with marketing to age. So what exactly does one need to do to get started? First and foremost, you will need to shake up the misconceptions that contribute to your organization's conventional philosophy. For starters, you will need to stop believing that an older consumer is less valuable than a younger one; the Gold Rush analogy is being used for a well-justified reason. You will also need to dispense with the bias of believing that it's better to build a franchise on a foundation of youth. Successful and enduring brand equities are built on a foundation of consumer loyalty, not age. Lastly, get over the hang-up that older people are not fashionable. Fashion is in the eye of the beholder, and when the Boomers look in the mirror, they like what they see. If they're happy, then you should be too.

In every marketplace, there are leaders and followers, and each group succeeds in its own way. The followers choose to be followers because where they may lack vision and initiative, they have exceptional ability to innovate the established category norm to add meaningful incremental value. In the case of the Old Rush, it's a call for leaders only. Remember, we're not talking about simply entering a new category here. We're referring to an emerging, unexploited aging marketplace and the opportunity to capture and hold significant market share by getting there first. That's an endeavor that requires the stuff that leaders are made of, along with the courage to dream. If the norm in most of today's mature businesses is survival of the fittest, then the best way to think about the Old Rush is, "Success of the first". It's time to get started while there are still big, shiny nuggets of opportunity waiting to be discovered.

Now that we've bolstered our understanding of how and why the Boomers are aging to perfection, it's time to step out of the realm of consumer marketing to see what we can learn from *things* that get better with age. Just as the history of the Gold Rush gives us a different way to think about the Old Rush, let's see if we can find insight into the aging process of everyday things. If you don't think that wine, cheese, leather, cast-iron skillets, and memories have anything in common, think again. Each improves with age but not because of age itself. There are myriad factors beyond the passage of time that influence how we perceive improvement in aging, and understanding them will be invaluable in your pursuit of creating marketing that gets better with age. So let's get started, beginning with a noteworthy glass of perfectly aged wine.

Cheers to our future success!

PART
TWO

*Things that Get
Better with Age*

SLOW AND STEADY WINS THE RACE

Moving slowly in your old age is par for the course, but if you're Jonathan the tortoise, the oldest living land animal, that's just the speed he's always walked. Living on the small island of St. Helena in the South Atlantic Ocean since 1882, Jonathan has lived through two world wars and numerous territorial skirmishes. He is thought to be at least 183 years old, only defined by many historical pictures discovered over the years with various soldiers of those many wars.

Jonathan is of the species *Testudinidae Cryptodira*, which has been known to live well into two centuries, and from the looks of Jonathan, he's not going anywhere fast. For many years his diet was not adequate for a tortoise his age, causing his "beak" to become soft and problematic for longevity, but recently his new caretaker adjusted his diet and he's looking as spry as ever.

Living in such seclusion on a small island has limited Jonathan's ability to mate and create young, but it's early days as yet for this gentleman - he's got many years to go.

CHAPTER
═══════ SEVEN ═══════

Wine

I was born in 1959, a year that would go down in wine annals as one of the greatest vintages ever. If wine were to be predictive of my life, it would seem I was born with great promise and a destiny to get better with age.

Perhaps I have been subconsciously inspired by my birth year, as I have a profound passion for wine. Not a glass of wine, per se, but all things wine. If you take the time to understand what's beyond the liquid in your glass, you'll discover that wine has deep roots. Roots that meander back to its origins in the agriculture and civilization of ancient China in 7,000 BC, its sacred place in religious rituals, and ubiquitous and seemingly essential presence in today's social and culinary pursuits, notably with people of age who have grown to appreciate fine wine over a lifetime.[36] Wine has been described in many ways, but to me, a great glass of wine is like poetry, a rhythmic collection of beautiful elements left open to personal interpretation.

While I'm not entirely sure where the inspiration hit me to write this book, there's a reasonably good chance that I saw the light over a glass of old, dark wine. Behold the power of wine – when it comes to symbols associated with positive aging, nothing else conjures up glorious improvement over time like fine wine. This rich metaphor is so universally accepted that no treatise on marketing to age would be complete without a deep understanding of the parallels between wine that gets better with age and people who see themselves improving with age.

Understanding what to make of wine begins with understanding how it's made. While the process of winemaking can be complex, in its simplest form it is about two things: agriculture and art. The agricultural piece is about the growing of great grapes that are the foundation for fine wine. This is where nature dominates and humans compensate. The art piece pertains to what *we* can impart to wine through the craft of winemaking that begins with having the honed instincts to know when it's best to harvest the fruit, combined with the deft skill of transforming the fruit into juice that can age to perfection.

When it comes to the practice of growing the grapes that go into the finest wines in the world, the concept of *terroir* is central. Terroir is French for "earth and soil", and terroir in wine refers to the specificity of the place where grapes are grown, the set of geographic, geological, and climate factors that interact with grapes to produce taste characteristics unique to that place. While sturdy grape varietals like Cabernet Sauvignon thrive in a broad range of growing environments, other more delicate varietals, like Pinot Noir – the grape behind noble red wines from Burgundy – require very specific conditions compatible with its needs and can ultimately coax out the unique brilliance of the fruit. The greatest wines in the world start with spectacular fruit grown in vineyards with exceptional terroir.

Winemaking is a refined art. It begins with assessing the quality of the harvested fruit, which in any given parcel varies year to year based on the actual pattern of weather during the growing season. For a given producer or Chateau, the technique with which each vintage is produced remains relatively consistent to be representative of their trademark style. However, it must also vary somewhat to compensate for the variables in the fruit from one vintage year to another.

At its most basic level, wine consists of fruit, tannins, acid, and sugar. A great winemaker uses the fruit nature provides and then applies craft to achieve a beautiful balance of these four elements.

When it comes to the great old vintages that have inspired this chapter, the element of wine that matters most is tannin. Tannin provides the essential structure, or integrity, that allows wine to age over time. Tannin comes from the seeds, stems, and skin of the grape. Wine also derives tannin from the oak barrels in which it's aged. As wines ages, the tannins soften, producing the elegant, silky, and velvety taste profiles associated with beautifully aged wine. To make a wine that will improve over time, tannin management is paramount to all other aspects of wine craft.

Most of the wine that we drink is produced to be consumed young – within a year of harvest. To some extent, drinking wines young is characteristic of the varietal itself; some wines simply don't require aging to be at their best. That said, the real reason that most wines are consumed without significant aging has to do with the fact that winemaking is a business. The aging of wine adds expense to the cost of goods in terms of input materials (expensive oak barrels), extended storage and handling time before release, and the deferral of revenue that is critical to offset sunken production costs. With the demand for wine at an all-time high, for these reasons and more top growers are producing quality wines more efficiently and getting them poured more quickly than ever. We live in times that demand immediate gratification – the wine industry is only too happy to please.

With all of the hype that surrounds aged fine wine, you might be surprised to learn that only 1% of all wines sold are suitable for extended cellaring and aging.[37] When you consider how deeply engrained the ethos of fine wine is, it's remarkable that the legendary allure of old wine can be propagated by so few bottles. Remarkable, that is, until you come to truly appreciate the 1% of wines responsible for the sensationalism.

While there are many brilliant examples of fine wines from every corner of the world, none are more coveted than the exquisite First Growth and Grand Cru wines from the Bordeaux and Burgundy regions of France. In a country celebrated for its rich tradition of winemaking, these are its two crown jewels. Bordeaux and Burgundy wines are perpetually in high demand, particularly if they are from a parcel designated as a First Growth or a Grand Cru. When perfect growing conditions are added to this equation, the resulting vintages are priced stratospherically, limiting their ownership not just to the wealthiest wine lovers in the world, but to those who have the money and inside access to highly limited distribution. Thus, an exceptional product is made virtually unattainable because of limited supply and excessive demand.

There is no better example of this than the wines of Domaine de la Romanée-Conti (DRC), an estate located in Burgundy. Wine from its namesake vineyard – Romanée-Conti – has the outright claim as being the scarcest, most expensive, and best wine in the world.[38] It is, in every sense of the word, true perfection in wine. While some would like to attribute the exceptional quality of this wine to DRC's remarkable terroir – limestone soil rich in iron on well-drained east- and south-east facing slopes – there are adjacent parcels that benefit from the same terroir and that produce wines every bit as exquisite in their own right but don't nearly begin to fetch the prices that DRC does. Why? The simple laws of supply and demand, made complex. Simple in that the DRC vineyard only produces 450 cases of wine on average per year – an extremely low supply for a product sought worldwide.[39] It's complex in that the demand side of the equation is driven by myriad human desires that start with the sensorial delight of its brilliant taste, but also includes all the unexpressed egotistical desires to own an object of status not available to others. This is what I was alluding to earlier when I spoke of "all things wine".

Noteworthy old wine comes from essentially two places: it is bought young and patiently aged in one's private cellar, or it is purchased as old wine at a high-end retailer or auction house. In either event, the owner has invested time, money or both in the wine, and has a material interest in seeing it improve with age. Now consider that this desire to own and drink nice wine lives within the broader cultural ethos of wine, one where the mystique of terroir, seductive parlance, and the pedigree of vintage have been romanced for centuries. To own but one bottle of this offers one great richness, measured either by the promise of a great occasion yet realized, the satisfaction of owning a piece of history or, as has become more of the norm of late, the conspicuous status of enjoying something so few can. If you roll all of this up, you begin to appreciate the meaning of "all things wine", but you also may come to realize that a lot of (too much?) deep meaning is being attached to old juice made from grapes. The moral of the story is that when you become invested in aged fine wine – either by ownership or by attachment to the mystique – you have a vested interest in seeing the scenario play out as desired.

So let's answer the question of how wine gets better with age, while drawing some parallels to marketing to age. Remember that while wine is a perishable commodity capable of deteriorating, that which preserves it is also what improves it: the complex interplay of sugars, acids, and phenolic compounds like the aforementioned tannins. If the wine is made and stored properly, and the chemistry of the wine goes as planned, the resulting bouquet, color, taste, and mouth feel are *deemed* to be more pleasant than that of a young wine.

The choice of the word "deemed" is deliberate and here's why. What goes on inside a barrel or a bottle of wine gracefully aging in the cellar of a French chateau is chemistry. That's right, chemistry. The elements of the wine and its environment are interacting with each other as part of an intended transformation of the wine. While we have romanticized the aging of wine, at the end of the day it's a technical process. Winemaking results in a formula of compounds that work synergistically to yield something different than what was originally placed in the barrel or bottle.

In this sense, the aging of wine does not categorically improve it, it simply changes it. The "improvement" that we claim to recognize in aged wine is the result of the positive perceptual associations that we bring to the tasting experience, which in turn are influenced by the ethos of wine, the mantra of which is "old wine tastes better". Let's repeat that for clarity. Aged wine doesn't technically improve, it technically changes. We attribute positive qualities to this technical change because we are influenced by the mental paradigm that we bring to the tasting of the wine.

While the basic premise of this book is that the aging consumer believes they're getting better with age, the *technical* truth is that they are not. In the same way that we perceive that wine improves with age, the Boomers are bringing their positive ethos of aging ("aging is good") to the interpretation of their technical reality. They have changed with age, and because the reality of that change is inconsistent with their desired scenario of life, they have created a new mystique that glorifies aging in all the ways that we've spoken of thus far in the book.

If you're marketing to age, the message here is that it's not what's in the bottle that counts, it's what you bring to the interpretation of what's inside. Just as wine is poetry – beautiful elements that are open to personal *interpretation* – so too is aging. The physical elements or words of aging aren't beautiful per se, but it's the nature of the human spirit to embellish reality, to create poetry out of life's advanced years that's pleasing to the soul. You're going to need to think outside the bottle and get inside their souls.

Another takeaway from our discussion of winemaking is that great wine begins with great grapes. The Boomers believe that they have improved with age because their lives have borne the beautiful fruit of hard work and success. They believe in the basics and fundamentals of life at a time when rampant innovation is challenging their notion of stability, permanence, and order. They believe that the best measure of one's character is one's actions, and that apropos of wine, what you get out of life is a function of what you put into it. To market to them you need to lead with substance and quality, wrapped up in a message of authenticity. Simply put, they won't drink your "wine" because you've found an enticing way to serve it up; you'll likely need to demonstrate that it was made with quality ingredients as part of a purpose dedicated to making things the right way. Nothing sells a Boomer like enduring quality, the epitome of the most classical wine producers in the world.

These same "classical" producers have found a way to balance traditional methods with innovative techniques, which by parallel, is an imperative for modern marketers. The Boomers have traditional roots and tendencies, but they are also embracing "innovation" to preserve a feeling of being vital in a changing world. This innovation can take the form of trying new ways of doing things or doing things never done before, just as easily as it could be the adoption of new smartphone technology to help one feel current in a world of innovation. As a marketer to age, you will need to fully understand the traditional and innovative tendencies of Boomers, and once you have, you will need to blend traditional and innovative marketing processes and techniques to reach them effectively. Many marketers have failed by assuming that the aging consumer is one-dimensional and bringing only a traditional outlook to their world, just as many have over-corrected by offering up innovation that is not grounded in tradition.

Lastly, and perhaps most importantly, the aging of fine wine takes endless patience. Aging is about the passage of time, and time takes time. Do all that you can to resist the pressure of our results-oriented, instant-gratification world. Marketing to age, and doing it successfully, is a process that will take time. If you are new to it, it may take a couple of "growing seasons" until your seeds bear the fruit you will need to produce an exceptional result. What you grow in one year may not grow the same the following year, but if you bring craft and diligence to marketing, you can compensate for variability in the marketing mix. Remember that marketing to age – like the making of a fine wine – is an art, and when you get it right, you will have created beautiful poetry that can't be resisted.

CHAPTER
═══ EIGHT ═══

Leather

Leather is the real deal. It's hard to think of any other natural material that is so ubiquitous and has such diverse, expressive power. Its perceived origin in the American West evokes the rugged individualism and masculinity of hard-working cowboys. When worn on the runways of New York and Paris, leather is a timeless fashion statement, and when seen on the big screen, adorning the backs of entertainment icons like James Dean, Marlon Brando, or Dennis Hopper, it's a universally accepted expression of individuality and rebellion. Want to get noticed? Wear more leather.

We love our leather, and our leather loves us. When cared for properly and used with love, it has its own intimate way of saying thanks by aging beautifully and getting better by the year. Our relationship with our cherished leather goods is unlike so many of the other things we own. Leather is deeply personal, it has a power over us, and at its best, it's totally seductive. When we shop for leather, it's a physical, visceral experience. We must touch it, handle it, and fondle it. We must smell it before running a hand over it to caress its smooth, shiny surface. We can't take our eyes off of it, and it takes great willpower to put it down and walk away. Great leather is incredible and, to many, it's almost irresistible.

Just thinking of leather stirs the senses. I was recently planning a trip to Madrid when I came across a description of an ancient sherry bar – La Venencia – that's tucked into the side of a narrow street in the heart of the city. I was intrigued for lots of reasons, not the least of which was that stepping into a well-worn bar like this would be like stepping into history, some of it shared with Ernest Hemingway. But what really got me was the description of La Venencia's interior as a timeless space that smells like the inside of an old leather briefcase. My lack of fondness for sherry did not deter me from visiting – I went just the same, and took in every delicious moment of the place. Each breath was a seduction of the senses, and delighted with a smell that I will never forget – one of centuries-old wood blended with the aromatics of vintage sherry that rolled itself up into a delicious, musky whiff of the best leather bag that one could only dream of owning.

While we've always loved our old leather, it's fair to say that today's aging consumer loves it more passionately than ever. If you spend as much time with aging consumers as we do, you quickly pick up on the themes and undercurrents that influence their commentary on life. Right up there with the most popular streams of thought on topics like technology and values is the aging consumers' disappointment with the degradation of quality in today's products. In a world where wood and metal have been gradually replaced by plastic and other synthetics, natural products like leather that have endured unchanged in a rapidly changing world are looking better than ever in contrast to a backdrop of imitation and compromised quality. Leather is still great after all these years.

Isn't it interesting that in a world where everyone loves that which is new, we find ourselves helplessly in love with something that's old? So how is it that leather actually gets better with age, and how might this inspire our efforts to get better at marketing to age?

First, leather gets better with age because it develops a patina. Patina refers to the accumulated changes in the texture, color, and appearance of leather that result from use over time. The elements and conditions that do the most to affect change in leather are wear, sunlight, moisture, heat, humidity, natural skin oils, and dirt. In that different leathers come from different rawhide and differing combinations of the above patina-creating conditions are in play, no two leather items age alike. Each has a patina totally unique to the item and the particular way the owner has used it.

For many items that we own, the above conditions would contribute to deterioration in their quality, not an improvement. A favorite cashmere sweater, lovingly worn and cared for, is eventually going to stretch and pill to the point where it ends up looking just like what it is — an old sweater. The difference with leather is that patina adds to the sensuality of its appeal. The patina that results from the oxidation of metals (think statues) is not always attractive, but a well-patinated piece of leather is almost always going to be gorgeous.

I recently refurnished the den in my antique home, and naturally, I was in the market for a leather couch. Restoration Hardware had some beautiful pieces to choose from, but none could compare to the vintage sofa that had once done time in a London pool hall. It goes without saying that I was drawn to its gothic design and sense of place, but when I laid eyes on its stunning patina, I was entranced. My mind took what I was seeing and ran with it. Clearly the tobacco brown color and luster was the making of years and years of use and the layered application of both spirit and spirits, with a dash of cue chalk thrown in for good measure. My family and friends are quick to tell me that my beloved London Pool Hall sofa is the most uncomfortable piece of furniture in the house, but no matter, because to me, it's the most beautiful one too.

Just as patina makes leather better by showing the accumulated effects of time, aging consumers' lives have provided layers of richness that are only now being fully appreciated. A young person is prone to think that aging produces wrinkles, but aging people see aging in an entirely different way — they see the beautiful patina of a life well lived. Their patina is not external; instead, it's the satisfaction of knowing that they've accomplished most of what they set out to do in life, and if they didn't, at least they've come to terms with it by now. They're enjoying contentedness and piece of mind, and most are pleased with where they are in life. They're proud of what they've accomplished, and their life's purpose is coming into the picture. Older, wiser, better? You bet.

Leather also gets better with age because it softens with use and its fit and form improves over time. This is often called the "breaking in" process, a description of the efforts that go into intensifying use to accelerate the affect. Have you ever rode in a new saddle or hiked in a new pair of boots? Neither is comfortable and the result is definitely not pretty.

Naturally, a lot has changed since my childhood, and since we're on the topic of leather, let's talk about my first baseball glove. Think 1964, a day and age when the name Hubbell would always prompt a stranger to ask if I was related to Carl Hubbell, the major league pitcher who became famous for striking out Murderer's Row – five of the game's best hitters, including Ruth and Gehrig – in succession at the 1934 All-Star game. Today I'm asked if I have anything to do with the Hubble space telescope.

My dad had been a pitcher in his day and, as was usually the case back then, my first baseball glove was a hand-me-down, but it came with a dividend – it was already broken in. Boy I loved that glove, but I eventually outgrew it and soon found myself struggling to get my new Rawlings mitt to resemble something that would actually bend when my fingers bent. Today's "shelf-ready" gloves are pre-treated to be ready for use, but back then, the breaking-in process was an all-consuming routine. First you would grind (and grind and grind) a ball into the perfect pocket within the pocket of the glove, continuously applying layers of neatsfoot oil, an oil rendered from the shinbones and feet of cattle. Once the pocket was formed, it was time to shape the glove around the ball by stretching it and then tying it up to hold and mold the leather in place. We would then put the tied-up glove in a random hot place like the attic, and eventually (one hoped) it would be ready to be put into action where actual use would allow the affects of moisture, skin oil, and dirt to finalize its aging. When baseball season ended, we moved on to breaking in our hockey skates. So it went.

Whether it's a pair of gloves or a pair of shoes, using leather improves it over time because the leather eventually conforms to the unique shape of an individual's foot or hand, hence the expression "it fits like a glove". The cashmere sweater we described earlier gets old quickly because it loses its shape over time. On the contrary, leather finds its shape and stays in shape. In this sense, leather is customized to one's individual characteristics – the item becomes personalized, and the owner's relationship with an object gets very intimate over time.

The Baby Boomers are a generation that yearns for more personalization and customization in the products and services they use. On the one hand, this demand is created by supply – manufacturers' improved ability to efficiently deliver mass-customized offerings. However, it's also hard-wired into Boomers' expectations because they grew up in a society that catered to their needs, whether it was suburban homes with yards and swing sets, cool cars for the new roads, Pepsi instead of Coke or even Lite beer when calories became an issue. They came of age in an era of unprecedented prosperity and the birth of modern marketing. They formed a set of personal values – including the belief that they could get what they deserved – that persevere to this day and still do more to influence choices and behaviors than many other aspects of the modern marketing mix.

This desire for personalization is also a desire for fit. The aging consumer has spent a lifetime experiencing the true benefit of products that "fit" them better than other products. Marketing can be defined as many things, but the definition that's inspired by leather is that marketing is about creating a perfect fit between your product and the needs of consumers. The way you create the perfect fit is to get to a highly personalized understanding of the consumer, while always remembering that people change, and that what once fit them may no longer be their "size", especially as they age. To know them, you have to walk in their (leather) shoes.

The last way in which leather improves with age has to do with its authenticity and permanence, qualities that are becoming increasingly valued in a replacement-driven, disposable economy. Leather is authentic because it has natural origins and has usually been improved over time as a result of normal, authentic factors intrinsic to its use. With an onslaught of imported imitations like "pleather", real leather makes a statement when worn well – I'm authentic because I value the authentic things (and people) in my life.

Aged leather is also a symbol of permanence, as it's a manifestation of the owner's investment over time to care for valuable things properly. In a world that's changing before our eyes, where fashion trends and hemlines are in constant movement, leather is a rock. It's eternal because it endures at a time when so many other aspects of our lives do not.

When you look at the authenticity and permanence of leather against the backdrop of the aging consumers' lives, its appeal becomes even more pronounced. The authenticity of things like leather is especially meaningful at a time when aging people are worrying about core values like honesty, the sincerity of human relationships, and the compromising of integrity. They want marketers to treat them with authenticity, to represent them the way they see themselves, and to demonstrate that they understand that life gets better with age. In short, they're saying, "Let's get real." One of the more refreshing financial services campaigns of late was the

"Ask Chuck" campaign for Charles Schwab. It acknowledged the reality of the consumers' world by imploring the industry to have practical conversations about clients' real needs and dreams, in lieu of promises of owning vineyards and sailing the world with wind in your hair during your blissful years of retirement.

The permanence of leather reminds us that the aging consumer also values permanence at a point in time when they have fewer years left to live than they have already lived. As their quantity of life decreases, they are offsetting it with an emphasis on quality of life, with a vengeance. While they may be aged, they are feeling and acting like they are ageless.

In summary, leather gets better with age because it develops a pleasing patina, it conforms to the unique personal characteristics of the owner, and it's a symbol of authenticity and permanence – the longer you own it, the more it says about your personal values. When you combine all of these aspects of aged leather, the implication for marketing to the aging consumer is pretty clear. They intend to age naturally, getting more beautiful by the year while reminding the world that they've been around long enough to achieve the reward of feeling comfortable with who they are. If that statement feels like a rebellion against aging, then so be it. There's a little bit of James Dean in all of us, even after all these years.

CHAPTER
═══ NINE ═══

Cheese

Everyone loves cheese, but no one can agree on its origins. Ancient records would suggest that early cheesemaking began over some 4,000 years ago, which certainly qualifies cheese as an appropriate subject for a book on age.

The earliest cheesemaking likely occurred in the Far East and spread to Europe from there. Cheese was soon made in many parts of the Roman Empire, and at one time, Italy became the most influential cheesemaking country in Europe, circa the 10th century.[40] It didn't take long for cheese to flourish as a cross-cultural food in Europe, and soon it made its way west once again as part of the foodstuffs of the Mayflower pilgrims.[41] Given that farming was the way of life in the New World, the early settlers had ready-access to fresh milk and were able to continue the tradition of cheesemaking in a new locale. This explains why states like Vermont continue to have such enduring cheesemaking traditions, and as subsequent waves of immigrant farmers made their way to the more arable soil of the midwest, it did not take long for states like Wisconsin to develop such rich reputations.

When we think of aged cheese, most of us probably think of cheddar, and if it's cheddar, it's probably from one of the two aforementioned states (did you know that cheddar cheese is named for the village of Cheddar in Southwest England where it was first made?). Brands like Cabot and Cracker

Barrel market extensive offerings of cheddar, varying by provenance, color, sharpness, and age. All of it is aged differently, ranging from one to two months for mild cheddar to a year or even 12 or more for exceptional cheddars.[42]

To learn more about how cheese improves with age, we're going to leave the pastoral setting of Vermont and cross the Atlantic to the cultural capital of the Netherlands – home to one of the finest aged cheeses in the world.

The city of Amsterdam perches majestically and magically where land and sea mingle. Without dikes to hold back waters, there would be no land. Without land on which to build, there would be no city. Water and city live together as harmoniously today as they have for over 800 years, preserving a bejewelled piece of geography and a treasured way of life.

Yet the magic of Amsterdam is not limited to its breath-taking setting, nor to its meandering waterways, its centuries-old houses and warehouses nestled side-by-side, nor to its jangling cacophony of busy bicyclists. Rather, magic is created every day by the mercantile genius of the Netherlanders. Ancient trades ascend to modern heights in this country, none more revered than the cheese that is virtually synonymous with Netherlanders: Dutch Gouda.

If you're looking for one of the best examples of this storied cheese, go no further than the intersection of Singel and Oude Leliestraat on the Singel canal. There you will find an old 17th century townhouse that is home to the world-renowned Reypanaer cheese, run for generations by the founding Wijngaard family. There you are sure to find a proud cheesemaker, one who is eager to share his knowledge of the Reypanaer way of making fine Gouda that gets better with age.

While all cheeses are made differently, the underlying art and science of cheesemaking is generally the same. The cheesemaker's job is to convert a type of milk into a type of cheese that exhibits consistent taste, texture, and aromatics from batch to batch; this process consists of culturing, coagulating, draining, and ultimately aging.[43]

The culturing process begins by heating the milk to a temperature that promotes the growth of bacteria capable of converting the milk's lactose into lactic acid, a process familiarly known as fermentation. In cheeses made with unpasteurized milk, the bacteria are "wild" and are already present. Alternatively, bacteria can be added to the milk from a culture or a starter bacterium. The process of fermentation creates compounds that lend unique taste characteristics to the cheese that reflect the unique nature of the bacteria culture. As an interesting side note, Emmenthal (Swiss cheese) gets its trademark holes from the gases created from a specific type of culture not used in fully solid cheeses like cheddar.

Once the fermentation is complete, an ingredient known as rennet – a complex of natural enzymes – is added to cause the proteins in the fermented milk to solidify, or in cheesemaking parlance, curdle.[44] Once the milk is sufficiently coagulated, the cheesemakers' next task is to remove most of the naturally occurring water (whey) from the milk. While this step is called draining, it essentially involves the dehydration of the milk, converting it into a curd.

At this point, the curd is ready to be aged into cheese, a step that differs by type of cheese, but essentially requires the management of temperature and humidity and the addition of mold spores that give rise to fungi (are we still hungry?).[45] In layman's terms, the mold creates biochemical changes that give each cheese its own distinct taste and aroma.

If you were to visit Reypenaer, your tour would take you to a solid yet beautiful warehouse where the practiced art of aging this exceptional Gouda has taken place for over a century. Like the cheese itself, this is an aged building. It is crafted of stone, brick, and timber, standing three stories above the waterway, with the inimitable style and sturdiness that define classic Dutch mercantile edifices. Arched windows allow light, temperature, and humidity to flow into the warehouse. Wooden shutters can be opened or closed as needed to modulate the interior environment. No modern air conditioning or other artificial means are used here; only traditional techniques in which nature is honoured and enabled to age the cheese to perfection over time.

Tall columns of Reypenaer Gouda are stacked in rows upon rows of wooden racks, and warehouse workers can be seen milling about, checking on and caring for each wheel of Gouda by hand. Some of these workers have been with the Wijngaard family for decades. Their touch and senses of taste, sight, smell, and even hearing, are able to discern exactly what care and conditions each wheel needs to be its best. Factories can make cheese edible. Only people can make cheese become exceptional.

If you were to follow a worker throughout the towering racks of cheese, you would see him periodically stop to randomly tap a wheel with a small hammer. His educated ear deciphers the pitch of each thump to determine how the aging is progressing. With other wheels of Gouda, he might massage them all over with his hands to encourage consistent aging. With still others, he might sniff and prod them to determine from vast personal experience how they are maturing. If they need a bit more coolness yet humidity on this day, he may open a nearby window, allowing moisture to enter, while closing the shutters to daylight. Hour by hour, day by day, month by month, this care continues, until every round of Reypenaer Gouda ages to its optimal maturity. Over a year's time, it can drop one-quarter of its original liquid weight. But this loss of water is not really a loss, for the more solid the Gouda becomes with age, the richer and tastier is its consistency.

Among the racks, you will find wheels of Reypenaer's V.S.O.P. and X.O. Reserve, the latter being their finest example of aged Gouda, the King of Reypenaer. Three years of masterful aging reveal a Gouda with crystalline studded creaminess, and complex, almost intoxicating flavors and textures that set X.O. Reserve on the highest possible pedestal. It is stunning proof that great cheese can become exceptional with age.

So now that we're craving a bite of Reypenaer's glorious aged cheese, what on earth does cheese have to do with our hunger to learn more about marketing to age? First and foremost, Reypenaer's Gouda gets better with age not because it gets old but because it ripens. What the cheese trade refers to as "aging" is actually a process of ripening.

Marketing is full of examples where the original language associated with an item is morphed to overcome an inherent negative. Patagonia Toothfish became Chilean Sea Bass, Spider Crabs became Snow Crabs, and "ripened" – a term associated with fruit or pungent spoilage, has become "aged" to add wine-like caché to cheese.

As we have consistently remarked, the Boomers do not see themselves as aging; instead, they are simply changing, and as they move through life, their view of life changes to support their desire to improve with age. While there's a bias to think of consumers over the age of 49 as being past their prime, the Boomers believe that they are only now just approaching their prime years. In this sense, the ripening (vs. aging) metaphor from cheese is very apt.

Therefore, you need to think about the Boomer consumer the way that Reypenaer thinks about Gouda: they are not aging, they are ripening. Ripening is about getting better with the natural passage of time. Things that ripen continue to grow and improve day by day. They are gradually transforming – almost imperceptibly at times – but they are on a predetermined path to reach a glorious state of achievement when they will be at their best. They will have ripened to their full maturity.

We have chosen Reypenaer to exemplify perfection in aging because their approach to cheesemaking offers other consistencies with respect to the aging consumer. Notably, they both honor heritage. When the founder of the Reypenaer Cheeserie, Piet Wijngaard, first established his trade in cheese, he also established a way of making Gouda that has been preserved for generations. When you look at the Baby Boomer generation, you see a cohort of consumers that has preserved its values for decades, irrespective of age or stage in life. Their values have been their enduring "heritage" of a sort, helping them stay true to their personal beliefs about the way the world and their lives should be. As they age, their "heritage" takes the form of their life experiences and the essential wisdom that has been gleaned from them, wisdom that breeds the confidence and self-satisfaction that are key catalysts for ripening into one's fullest potential. Aging consumers are living in their prime years because their heritage – an accumulation of life experiences – has prepared them for "prime time".

There's yet another parallel between aged cheese and aged people. Aging solidifies Gouda. My grandfather used to say, "By the time you figure it all out, you run out of time." True of life, but also true of many of life's experiences. If you've ever been to Disney World, you'll remember that first day in a new "world" and what it felt like to be so immediately overwhelmed by the physical and human scale of the place. But as the week goes on, and your familiarity with your surroundings improves, so does the pleasure that you derive from the experience. Because your knowledge of your setting has improved, you have "figured it all out". Just as you are feeling as though you have mastered Disney World, it's suddenly your last day and it's time to go home.

Your knowledge of Disney came together over time and solidified. It felt good to have a firm understanding of life at Disney World. Now translate this metaphor to the life of an aging consumer. Their sum total of life experiences has solidified their understanding of the "ways of the world", which helps them derive more pleasure from each day. They are at a stage in their lives that felt as good as your fifth day at Disney.

Lastly, aging cheese at Reypenaer is a hands-on endeavor. To their way of making cheese, there is simply no substitute for a physical, tactile relationship with the cheese to get to a deeply personal understanding of its condition. If you are going to market to age, you are going to need to be just as "hands-on" with the aging consumer. If you intend to touch their lives with your product or service, you are going to need to find a way to physically touch their lives.

While it's easier to read research summaries in the comfort of your office or to eat M&M's and poke fun at the consumer behind the physical barrier of a focus group mirror, there simply is no substitute for visiting a consumer's home or going shopping with him or her. I've just come off a week of three-hour in-home visits for one of my clients. As an agency CEO with a very full plate, it would have been incredibly easy for me to justify sending someone else. Instead, I opted for the "hands on" learning experience, and once again, I was blown away by the depth of understanding that I accumulated, but more importantly, the genuine empathy I developed for the consumer's life and the role of the produce in improving it. There were moments when I felt like I was tapping the cheese and interpreting the sound.

Our "visit" to Reypenaer has been enriching as it has helped us to appreciate their timeless methods of making aged cheese. Cheese that ripens to perfection is flavored through a respect for heritage and solidifies over time. This is the life of aging consumers, a life that is a natural process oriented to improvement over time, if not perfection. If you are going to improve the way that you market to them, you will need to understand the true flavor of their lives. Like some of the world's finest foods, they will tantalize you with layer upon layer of vexing complexity, but when you do finally decipher the right ingredients of the marketing mix, you will own a treasured recipe for the sweet taste of success.

CHAPTER
TEN

Memories

Memories make us who we are. On a primal level, being able to remember who we are, who others are, what's dangerous, and what isn't are critical to our survival. Memory underpins everything we have ever thought or learned throughout our existence.

On a daily basis, memory is essential to getting us through the day, helping us remember to do basic instinctual things like thinking, walking, talking, and recognizing what's happening in our world. Memory is critical to our existence and it's important to marketers because it lies at the heart of cognitive psychology, the branch of psychology that seeks to understand mental processes and their effects on human behavior.

For the purposes of improving our understanding of the aging consumer, the memory that's most relevant is long-term memory or LTM. But before we go there, I must share a word or two on short-term memory – particularly the dreaded short-term memory loss – if for no other reason than to give the aging consumer a face-saving explanation.

Basic information, like telephone numbers and where you left your glasses, is stored in one's short-term memory (STM) after a brief trip through the sensory memory (SM), our immediate memory of what we see, hear, smell, taste, and touch.[46] The problem is that short-term memories only last for about 30 seconds, so in the event that you failed to make a conscious effort to commit the information to your LTM (as in, I wasn't really thinking about my glasses when I left them in the kitchen), it will be displaced by the next information that arrives in the STM.[47] Said another way, aging people have a lot on their minds and it's not really their fault that they're occasionally forgetful (as to the little things in life that don't really matter anyway).

Back to long-term memory. Unlike SM and STM, LTM is relatively permanent and has significant storage capacity, way more than we actually use in a lifetime.[48] The memories stored in our LTM are the memories that we remembered to process when they were in our STM. These memories have made a successful passage to the safekeeping in the LTM, either because we have attached some significance to them or we have repeated them sufficiently so as to be remembered.[49] Most of our recollections of life events and experiences – and how they made us think and feel – are permanently part of our LTM. Intriguing science if you're a marketer.

So to talk about memories getting better with age, we will be talking about long-term memories. These are the memories of things that occurred in the past that influence how aging consumers think and behave today. And remember, since an aging consumer has lived a longer life than a younger consumer, there is more memory at work influencing things like preference and choice. Just as the brain encodes memories, if we want to really understand these consumers, we will clearly need to do some decoding.

One of the more intriguing ways that memories improve with age is that they get "rewritten". Have you ever heard the phrase, "The older you get, the better you used to be"? Guilty as charged. Indeed, we all have a knack for embellishing the past and adding accomplishments to our personal "highlight reel" that may not have happened exactly as we describe them. No harm, no foul, right? We're simply romancing the story a little bit just to make it a little more interesting. The fact that everyone does this in some way suggests that there's something universal going on – something related to the cognitive psychology of memories.

According to recent research conducted by Northwestern Medicine and published in the *Journal of Neuroscience*, the very act of recalling a memory changes it.[50] In actuality, you aren't recalling the original memory, you're recalling a version derived from the last time you remembered it. Think of the implications – it's just like the old game of telephone. A memory from your childhood that's been recalled often gets progressively less accurate as a different version of it gets filed back in storage after each recollection. When you take the book off the shelf next time, it's like it's been rewritten.

Northwestern Medicine's lead researcher, Donna Bridge, described it as follows: "A memory is not simply an image produced by time traveling back to the original event – it can be an image that is somewhat distorted because of the prior times you remembered it. Your memory of an event can grow less precise even to the point of being totally false with each retrieval."

In that it's the tendency of a sane mind to be positive, it seems as though we are prone to adding glossy layers to our memories as we age. We may not actually be better than we used to be, but the only version of the memories that we are capable of conjuring up sure has us believing that the "good old days" were actually great.

The takeaway here is that a generation of consumers who grew up in an era of unprecedented optimism – and is thereby already prone to being positive – is subconsciously bolstering their positive outlook on life every time they recall the most potent memories of their lives. These are the same people who put a positive spin on aging to help make their current reality feel more pleasing. Aging consumers are brimming with positivity and on the lookout for more. Give them what they want by presenting your brand in a benevolent way that adds positivity to their lives. Too many brands make the mistake of thinking that they're doling out positivity when they offer up solutions to problems. It's clear that these folks aren't going to spend any time on negative memories when they're hardwired for positive.

On a related note, memories also get better with age because of the nostalgia effect. Nostalgia is a sentimental longing or wistful affection for happy associations with the past. The nostalgia effect pertains to how nostalgic memories affect the way we feel, and those feelings influence how we act. At its simplest, nostalgia is a good dose of medicine. Reminiscing about positive memories of the past gives us a boost of positive feeling in the present. In some instances, sentimental recall helps us cope with something unpleasant in our current life, eg. arthritis may have slowed you down but boy were you fast in that marathon you ran in college. In other cases, wistful thoughts of the past are conjured up instinctually as content to fuel our increasingly positive outlook on life as we age.

Yes, nostalgia is powerful stuff. It's no surprise that marketers have always strived to tap the power of nostalgia, wrapping their brands in a timeless kind of good feelings that gently tug at the open hearts of consumers. If nostalgic marketing has always been potent, imagine what happens when it's directed to an aging consumer who's getting more nostalgic by the year? Done well, it's priceless.

Nostalgic done well is something we call "nowstalgia", the art of making positive memories of the past relevant in the here and now. The essential aspect of this concept is relevance – the nostalgic endeavors that fail are almost always the ones that fail to translate the brand's past to the current day in a way that offers a current benefit that's relevant and interesting. Sure, we loved root beer growing up in the '50s and '60s, but nostalgic images of foamy-headed, draft-style root beer probably aren't going to be enough to get us to switch from the Diet Coke we're drinking today.

A brand that executes "nowstalgia" consistently well is Budweiser, by way of its enduring Clydesdale equity. A cynic could easily regard a horse-drawn beer wagon as an irrelevant relic of the past, but Budweiser has artfully found a way to make the image timeless.

They've done this in two ways. First, they have featured the Clydesdales as characters in timeless storylines. There's brutally simple but not obvious logic behind this. If there's a risk that horses pulling a beer wagon can be seen as old-fashioned – living in another time – then make them part of a story that knows no time – a timeless story. Case in point, the Super Bowl XLIX ad that won "best in show". It tugged at our hearts with a simple but timelessly potent storyline that featured the Clydesdales as heroes, fearlessly rescuing a wayward Dalmatian from wild wolves. Straight from a childhood storybook – pure nostalgia, but nothing old fashioned about it.

The second way they have made nostalgia relevant is by merging a traditional story with contemporary special effects. Who could forget watching the Clydesdales playing a game of football and kicking the extra points through two upright telephone poles as a pair of ranchers looks on? Modern filmmaking, timeless entertainment.

Marketers wanting to help Boomers live the good old days today might also want to think about appealing to their senses to trigger their memories. It's a scientific fact that no other sense triggers memory more readily than the olfactory sense – the sense of smell.

Who doesn't love that new-car smell? Guess what – it's not the leather seats, it's a seductive fragrance that's been added to your car to help you feel wonderful about your expensive new purchase. It's an aesthetic that confirms that you made a quality choice.

What about cologne and perfume? One would think that the popular fragrances from the Boomers' earlier years could be let out of the bottle again with new applications. If faux leather fragrance can make a car seem great, imagine what Calvin Klein could do for bed linens?

To a lesser but still significant extent is the emotive power of sound – the sound of music. Period music is enormously appealing to Boomers, but contemporary advertisers have been slow to use it. Used the right way, music from the Boomers' younger years elicits memories of the days when their lives were simpler and more carefree, which in turn creates more joy in the moment. What's more, music from their "good old days" signals that the advertiser not only understands them and their unique love of music, but cares enough about them to reflect this in their campaign.

Now is the time for a little more "nowstalgia" in marketing. While it might seem counterintuitive, taking aging consumers back in time may be just what you need to create timeless loyalty for a lifetime. That's a sentimental journey you're going to really want to think about going on.

The final way that memories get better with age has to do with life stories and legacies.

Stories are how we make sense of the world, our lives, and ourselves. Studies in personality psychology reveal that we translate the events, experiences, and relationships of our lives (preserved as memories) into on-going life stories that provide a narrative by which we understand our identity and role in society.

According to researcher Dan P. McAdams in the *The Handbook of Personality: Theory and Research:* "The stories we construct to make sense of our lives are fundamentally about our struggle to reconcile who we imagine we were, are, and might be in our heads and bodies with who we were, are, and might be in the social contexts of family, community, the workplace, ethnicity, religion, gender, social class, and culture writ large."[51]

These memory-inspired stories usually reflect one's morals and help to answer basic questions like, "Am I a good person? Have I led a good life?" At their best, they are a window into understanding our essence and true purpose in life. They afford us periodic glimpses in the mirror to help us confirm that we like what we see.

Our stories are a sort of moral compass that guide us through life, and as we grow older, we age into stages that have us looking at life differently. In *The Mature Mind*, Gene Cohen speaks about several stages of aging, notably the re-evaluation stage. This is the phase of life that many Boomers currently find themselves in. Having just experienced a major life change (think empty nest, divorce, leaving the traditional workplace), they are in a period of transition, which by necessity has them thinking about how best to answer the question of "What's next?" It is a stage often characterized by self-introspection, discovery, and personal quest. Many aging people are currently at a similar crossroads in their life. As they look for direction, they are turning to their life stories, a nearly complete narrative composed of chapter after chapter of memories. As one's life memories get woven into the fabric of their life stories, the memories get better because they are being put into the broader perspective of life, which gives them deeper meaning and purpose.

An important chapter in my life story is my memories of growing up on a dairy farm. These were difficult years, marked by constant hard work and subsistence living. Clearly nothing to be writing about all these years later. However, as the years have gone by, I have reinterpreted my recollection of these memories to make them more compatible with my full life story. When asked now, I tell folks that my years growing up on a farm taught me the value of hard work and instilled a work ethic that has helped me succeed in a challenging industry. Case in point – memories get better when they're read as part of a positive life story.

What is the role of legacy in making memories better? All of us are hardwired to give a darn about what we're going to leave behind when we're gone. It's why animals and humans focus on making babies to carry on with what they've started. When we think of legacy, we tend to think of grand accomplishments or great deeds that result in public recognition, but the reality is that most of us are influenced by simple motivations: to make sure that we're associated with having made a positive difference that might benefit those who follow.

While this is something that we all ponder as we meander through life, it's not until we reach our advanced years that we start to give the topic proper airtime. I must confess that I read the obituary section of the *New York Times* every day, not so much because I'm looking to see who has passed, but to see how they are being remembered. The headlines use as few words as possible to describe decades of life: John Bull, courageous D-Day veteran, appearing next to Flint Wilcox, bon vivant. Reading these condensations of life makes one wonder one of two things: how will they ever boil my life down into so few words, or more likely, have I done enough in my lifetime to fill up five words?

Our legacy is the title of our life story that's made up of chapters of memories. If a legacy is all about leaving something positive behind, we are going to reinterpret our memories as positively as we can. It's as instinctual as the primal instincts we were given to procreate to perpetuate life. This is pretty deep stuff, but at the end of the day, it's deep understanding that leads to the pithy insights that inspire great ideas in marketing. In contrast to the 18- to 49-year-old consumers who are the norm in marketing, the 49+ consumers exceed the norm. They have lived a longer life that has given them more time to shape a clearer sense of who they are and what's important to them. Marketers talk a lot about how important it is to align product benefits with consumer needs, and we love to draw Venn diagrams to help us identify the sweet spot where benefits intersect with needs. All of that is great, but if you've been tracking with the message of this chapter, it's not about understanding benefits and needs; it's about *aligning* with the aging consumer. Aligning with their memories, because after all, if it's memories that define who we are and that give our life meaning, the things we're trying to sell are going to seem trivial if they are not *aligned* with how aging consumers see their *own* lives, which in turn is about lifetimes of memories. Boy, does this sure give "Getting into the head of the consumer" a whole new meaning!

SPANNING TIME

The Caravan Bridge over the River Meles in Izmir, Turkey, is only 42.5 feet long, but the history of the river that it spans is deep as it has literary roots in Homer's work. The bridge looks like many of the other bridges in that area of the world with a fairly traditional look. Built in 850 BC, the Caravan Bridge is 2,861 years old and has stood the test of time and it is still in active use by the Turks of the area. Most of the bridges in the area have been destroyed and rebuilt or just left to fall apart letting the newer bridges pick up the traffic, but the Caravan Bridge still stands. A testament to engineering and pure luck, this grand little bridge endures as one of the oldest continuously used manmade objects in the world. Is anyone looking to buy a used bridge?

CHAPTER
ELEVEN

Cast-Iron Skillets

C ast-iron cookware is one of the most enduring fixtures in the culture of food preparation. Every professional chef and accomplished, knowledgeable home cook regards their cast-iron skillets, griddles, woks, and grill pans as among the most beloved and important stovetop tools they own. Many of the world's finest professional chefs have been known to bring their personal collections of cast-iron cookware with them when they open new restaurants. Only their knife collections receive the same level of fealty and life-long personal attention.

From its humble origins in the ancient world to its legendary presence in cowboy chuck wagons and frontier cook-tents to its nearly ubiquitous use in diners, grills, home kitchens, fine dining establishments, there is no other category of cookware that rivals cast iron when it comes to getting better with age.

Fashioned into a multitude of implements, this ancient metal has survived millennia as an indispensible cooking material. These days – in our highly specialized "foodie" culture – a well-seasoned cast-iron skillet, griddle, or grill pan is positively required for the "correct" preparation of such staple dishes as steak, hamburgers, bacon, lamb chops … even seared tuna. And, lest you think that cast iron is relegated to the savoury side of the menu, legions of top bakers still insist on vintage cast-iron bakeware to produce the best muffins, cakes, breads, and patisserie.

In China, home to one of the world's greatest and most revered ancient cuisines, the very finest hand-cast, hand-hammered iron woks – both professional and domestic – are typically handed down from generation to generation (more on this later). Some of these tools have been in near-constant use for more than two centuries. These tools bear the residual patina and inspire reverence comparable to the finest Stradivarius and Guarneri del Gesù violins of Cremona, Italy.

The very essence of cast iron's power to maintain an enduring presence in our global food culture is precisely rooted in the specific ways it gets better with age. Widely known for its extreme durability and heat retention, the real "magic" of a cast-iron skillet emerges, evolves, and is "perfected" over years – even decades – by what chefs and cooks call "seasoning".

When it comes to cast iron, the concept of seasoning has nothing to do with our traditional understanding of tastes and flavors. Technically, it is the process by which the porous, pebble-like surface of bare iron is permeated by baked-in layers of vegetable oils and animal fats until the cooking surface takes on a dark black veneer and virtually non-stick cooking quality. There is nothing complex about this. Seasoning a new cast-iron skillet is incredibly easy to do. Not surprisingly, the internet provides an endless number of tips, instructions, and how-to videos on the subjects of seasoning, care, and maintenance of cast-iron cookware.

For chefs and – even serious home cooks – seasoning is much more. It is a "term of art" that defines and describes the unique amalgamation of elements derived from the cook's own repertoire. Fats, salt, meats, starches, and innumerable other flavors are components of the alchemy. Each well-seasoned cast-iron skillet is custom "curated" by its user's own tastes, expertise, circumstances, and culinary proclivities.

These are then galvanized and caramelized by fire, time, and oxidation into layer upon layer of fine residual patinization that permeates the porous surface of the cast iron to make it — and the food prepared in it — an authentic expression of unique and timeless experience ... not unlike life itself!

The story of the processes and paths by which such a ubiquitous and simple product — fabricated from one of the oldest materials known to civilization — has emerged, evolved, and endured as an invaluable cooking instrument of the "global kitchen" offers important comparisons and analogies for marketers who need to understand how to think about, and message to, the tens of millions of aging Baby Boomers who are themselves getting better with age.

The earliest uses of cast iron in connection with the preparation of food are widely believed to date back more than two thousand years to the giant cauldrons used in Han Dynasty-era China to boil sea water into salt. In addition to cauldrons, covered cook-pots (predecessors to today's Dutch Ovens) and pots or woks attached to cast-iron legs to keep them suspended over an open fire (known as spider pots) were the predominant food preparation vessels across the world.

The introduction of the stove, which first appeared in post-Industrial Revolution Europe, moved cooking from the hearth to the kitchen. Soon after, the spider pot's legs were amputated to accommodate waist-level cooking, and the skillet was born.

It is interesting to note that unlike many of the things that get better with age discussed in this section — notably wine, cheese, and leather — the cast-iron skillet of 2015 is virtually the same in terms of design, manufacture, and use as the cast-iron skillet of 1815. Over the past several generations we have witnessed the ever-increasing power of human innovation and imagination to transform and improve virtually every aspect of our lives and everything we touch.

In the face of this irresistible force, very few things remain constant and unbent by the forces of innovation and market dynamics. The cast-iron skillet is one such thing. Is it because this simple tool is too pedestrian or too perfect? I will leave it for you to decide.

Cast iron was a ubiquitous presence in the American home kitchen during the first half of the 20th century. Griswold and Wagner Ware were the dominant brands in the category, and it is estimated that most American households owned at least one piece of cast-iron cookware during this period. Because they are virtually indestructible, it is not uncommon to find "vintage" Griswold and Wagner skillets still in everyday use across America. But it is more rare than you might think. Both Wagner and Griswold are long defunct, leaving Lodge Manufacturing as the major US-based maker and supplier of cast-iron cookware.

As might be expected, the now-defunct brands – particularly Griswold – have become legendary; and an amalgamation of anecdotal folklore has built up over the years among cast-iron mavens. This is particularly true for Griswold products manufactured prior to 1949. It seems that in that year, flush with post-war cash and optimism, the Griswold management made a large capital investment in new manufacturing equipment designed to scale up its efficiency and output. Of course, new molds, machine tools, and metallurgy were created to accommodate this new manufacturing technology. However, the resulting skillets and cook-pots were apparently far inferior to the pre-1949 versions fabricated with the older molds, machine tools, and metallurgical "recipe". It seems that the older manufacturing equipment and process yielded a product that was thicker and made of a denser, more porous base iron than the "new-fangled" ones. Of such stuff are legends made.

Before the end of the 1950s, Griswold and Wagner were both out of business as the nation transitioned to newer, lighter, and more convenient materials for cookware. But the legends of these brands continue to live on today. A quick check at eBay reveals a plethora of pre-1949 Griswolds and vintage Wagner Ware skillets on the secondary market. Depending on condition and provenance, these nearly antique, pre-seasoned (or "used") relics can fetch prices in excess of $150 for a 10-inch skillet. This is remarkable, especially if you consider that my recent visit to a well-known national home goods chain store found a brand new 10-inch Lodge skillet priced at $24.99, while a visit to a local restaurant-supply outlet unearthed an unbranded one − made in China − for $14.99.

In the 1960s and 1970s, both home cooks and professional chefs were ditching their ancient Griswolds and Wagners for new materials that promised better performance in terms of heat retention, even heat distribution and non-stickness … and which were much more attractive and appealing to the fashion-conscious homemaker of the period. French copper, stainless steel, and Teflon®-coated aluminium today lead the category. Brands such as All-Clad, Calphalon, and Cuisinart dominate retail shelves with products that occupy the high end of the cookware price-point range. Today, there are only a handful of lucky cooks whose mothers did not wantonly discard their antediluvian Griswolds in the 1950s and 1960s in favor of the modern-day miracle of Teflon®.

As an aside, I count myself among this fortunate subset, although not because my mother eschewed Teflon®. She did not. It was just her deeply ingrained Connecticut Yankee frugality that simply would not allow her to throw away what she regarded as a "perfectly good" skillet … even if she didn't use it anymore. Besides, we lived on a farm, and there was more than ample storage space in the attic and barn for the things my mother decided we would probably never need … but were still a "shame" to throw away.

Several manufacturers − most notably Staub, Tramontina,

Lodge, Copco, and Le Creuset – today sell cast-iron cookware that has been coated with a vitreous enamel glaze. The glaze eliminates the need for seasoning while preserving the heat retention properties of the cast iron. It also provides manufacturers with the opportunity to bring designer colors to the drab, utilitarian black patina of old-fashioned bare iron.

To experience first-hand how cast-iron cookware gets better with age in the context of modern-day commercial kitchens, I recently took two field trips to tour the cast-iron collections of two different restaurant kitchens. My objective was to get a first-hand perspective on how chefs use cast iron in today's food-obsessed culture, and specifically how its ability to get better with age influences and inspires their cooking.

My first destination was a Michelin-starred fine dining establishment on the Upper West Side of Manhattan whose chef-proprietor I will refer to as "Bob" (out of respect for his requested anonymity). Full disclosure: I have known Bob (who is a fellow Boomer, of course) for more than a decade and have patronized his restaurant many dozens of times in that period. I am something of a "regular" there.

While most of the saucepans, sauté pans and roasting cookware in Bob's kitchen are copper core clad in commercial-grade stainless steel, the Dutch ovens (used in preparation of slow-braised dishes), the bakeware (bread, cake, and pie "tins" plus cookie sheets) and a large stack of omelette pans were exclusively cast iron. Bob explained that the special properties that cast iron imparts to preparations such as yeast breads, pastry, slow-braised meats, and omelettes simply cannot be replicated by other surfaces. So he long ago decided to make the investment in owning and caring for specialized cast-iron cookware for these recipes and dishes. He told me that this is a cookware distinction that many restaurant owners do not make, and that is typically found in the kitchens of relatively expensive establishments. The average age of a piece of cast iron in Bob's kitchen is 25 years, which dates back to the founding of his first restaurant (the current place is his third), and he regards these venerable tools as among the most important aspects of his career success.

For another perspective on cast iron's place in the culinary world, I ventured into the kitchen of chef H. Liu (also a pseudonym) who oversees and co-owns one of the most highly regarded and innovative Chinese restaurants on the East Coast. A fourth-generation master chef, Liu's great-grandfather was among the most prominent chefs in Shanghai before the Maoist Revolution. His family escaped to Hong Kong, where he was born, before coming to the United States nearly 60 years ago. Chef Liu does not really know a life outside of the kitchen, but the reverence he has for food, and for the tools of his trade, is truly inspiring.

Liu said that the essence of food preparation lies in iron and steel: the steel of the blade and the iron of the wok. When I reminded him that I was there to talk about iron, he proudly showed me the six enormous (40-inch diameter) built-in, gas-fired, cast-iron woks that form the nucleus of his kitchen's stir-fry operation. They are finely seasoned from nearly three decades of constant use and careful maintenance ... slippery to the touch without being oily ... luminous like a black pearl and not the slightest bit gritty.

Liu remarked that for the first 10 years or so after the woks were installed, his food was not as good as it became after a decade of constant use. I could tell he was half joking, but only half. He then told me that most commercial woks in use these days in the United States are fabricated from stainless steel and have an average life of 20 years, while his, which are approaching their 30th "birthday", can last for another hundred years and will keep getting better.

After my deep dive into how cast-iron skillets (and woks) get better with age, I found myself hungry for some relevant implications, insights, and lessons for marketers who want to get better with aging consumers and tap into the lucrative and growing Boomer-driven longevity economy. The truth is that the takeaways for marketers are as simple and straightforward as a cast-iron skillet.

It is true that every well-seasoned cast-iron skillet (and wok) works in the same way, and it is equally true that every one is completely different. The absolute uniqueness of every skillet emerges over time as a result of both use and culinary proclivity. What is cooked, when it is cooked, how often dishes are prepared, and how the surface is cared for are all critical factors. After a lifetime of repeated use, every cast-iron skillet is still a cast-iron skillet, but no two are alike.

Similarly, while it's okay to generalize about what Boomers have in common (a Boomer is a Boomer), no two aging consumers are alike because each one of us has experienced a different life and has been influenced differently by our unique experiences. We may have grown up sharing many of the same values, but after a "lifetime of use", each of us has developed our own personal veneer that defines who we are. We all want to believe that we are getting better with age, but each of us is improving differently. Marketing – and especially targeting theory – has a tendency to generalize. Targeting consumers aged 18 to 49 with a single message fundamentally assumes that they are all alike. Aging consumers have been seasoned by life and true success in marketing to age lies in understanding their variability more so than their commonalities – the cast-iron analogy reminds us that it's not about the metal, it's about the seasoning.

We've also revealed that despite all of the modern advances in culinary tools and techniques, the cast-iron skillet remains a timeless classic. It is literally ageless. It's often a hand-me-down that endures from one generation to the next, providing it's unique "flavor" to foods and life alike, while also extending the legacy of its prior owners. While this dense metal tool is as inanimate as an object can be, it is simultaneously brimming with life because it has character, an endearing personality that is the patina of all who have used it to nurture loved ones with comfort food. Every time one uses a skillet that has been passed down from generation to generation, they're tasting a very special flavor that is unique to their family but it's also a taste that might momentarily connect them with all of their loving ancestral caregivers. It's hard to imagine any other single object that serves as a daily time capsule of family heritage. Family trees and photo albums don't bring the flavor of family to life the way a cast-iron skillet does.

The beauty of the cast iron skillet is that is has gotten better with age by changing, while not changing. This could not be a more apt description of Boomers themselves. They're embracing change as a dynamic that keeps everyday life interesting while keeping them current in an ever-changing world. Yet they simultaneously yearn to be anchored in aspects of permanence – things that have endured the way they want to see themselves endure in life. Things that have "been around a long time" are reassuring because more often than not, they serve as a bridge that spans our lifetimes and transports us back and forth from our carefree youth to our nostalgic current age. Cooking with cast iron is simultaneously traditional yet contemporary, not unlike the modus operandi of most aging consumers.

Finally, the story of cast-iron skillets reinforces the lesson that what's old becomes new again … and again … and again. Authenticity is enduring, and there is perhaps nothing as authentic as a cast-iron skillet, or as delicious as the "char" on a hamburger imparted by its well-used, well-seasoned surface. Cast iron has survived every culinary fad and then some, and is enjoying a renaissance because of its proven record of reliability. The Boomers are marketing's Most Valuable Generation™ because they have been a reliable source of brand loyalty for decades. Don't forsake them simply because they have aged or because you are tempted by other, younger generations. Our brief cookware analogy reveals how timeless some things can be, regardless of all the surrounding pressure to innovate. As coveted consumers, the Boomers are the original material; they've performed admirably for years and they've grown better with age. They are determined to endure, and when they set their minds to something, they almost always prevail. Make sure they're part of your recipe for growth.

PART
THREE

*Fifty Ways to Get
Better with Age*

You've made it this far, so it's fair to assume that you understand the need to get better with age and you're at least somewhat inspired by the illustrations and insights offered. All well and good, but where does one go from here? How do you take the first step in getting better at marketing to age, and once you do, how can you be sure that your journey will lead you to the right place? While we don't have a map for marketing to age, we can at least point you in the right direction and provide some markers to keep you on a course to success.

What follows are 50 (the only number that seemed appropriate for this topic) pieces of practical advice to help you initiate, plan, and execute a productive program for marketing to age. While some of these insights are specific to aging and others are more general in nature, all are intended to provide invaluable perspective for marketers who have the resolve to tap into this highly valuable emerging market. Don't be overwhelmed by their number, as they tend to be light reading renditions of poignant topics – with any luck, you might even find a few to be entertaining.

Please read on and absorb the wisdom that's here for the taking. You've aged somewhat since you started this book, but if you've come this far, you've definitely grown better with age and the best is yet to come.

EVERYTHING
BIG STARTS SMALL

O ur Agency recently picked up a small assignment
from a really big client and when I shared the
great news with some friends in the business, one
of them complimented me while also snickering
a bit about the size of the win. When I called him on it,
he confessed that at the big inter-galactic agency where he
works, they only chase really big accounts. I snickered back
when he wasn't looking.

Big business forgets that everything that is big today was once
small. One of my favorite expressions is: "Today's mighty
oak tree was once a stubborn acorn that stood its ground."
When you look up at the towering height and massive limbs
of a majestic oak, it's hard to believe that it started as a
miniature acorn, but it's true. Most things in life begin as
seeds, and if nurtured well in the right environment, they
grow and flourish. I get excited about the small assignments
that we win from big clients because I've lived long enough to
see big trees grow before my eyes. I have seen proof that all
big things start as small things.

The point of this book is to plant a seed called marketing
to age so you can watch your business flourish as others
search for growth elsewhere. The seed is the knowledge and
confidence that marketing to age is a smart and right thing
to do, and the planting of that seed is your willingness to put

marketing to age to the test in the marketplace. Because it's only a seed planted in a small area of your business, it's small. Most of us can get away with small because no one notices small in a world of big – not to mention that the consequences of failure are small. But since you believe that all things big start small, you will watch over your small seed to be sure it gets ample sunshine and nourishment and that the weeds of mediocrity are kept at bay. Since big takes time, you will also heed the importance of having a long-term outlook and abundant patience.

At some point, your seed will sprout and grow, gradually becoming more visible to others. If you continue to nurture it, it will grow beautifully, and it will soon become the envy of others who lacked the foresight to have planted a seed all those months ago. At this point, you will be able to step back and admire what you have brought into the world: a tangible, living, and glorious manifestation of your vision. Few things in life are as rewarding as the splendor of a great accomplishment, and in the world of business that seems to define our lives these days, they're farther and fewer between.

You need not be intimidated by marketing to age if you think of it simply as the planting of seeds. Companies today love to encourage their people to "think big", but in so doing, they end up aiming too high. Big starts small and you need to be sure to leave room in your process for small things to thrive, which shouldn't be hard because small things really don't take up that much room. If you're interested in pursuing the big opportunity of marketing to age, think small and you'll be amazed how quickly things will grow. Now that's a big idea.

AGE IS NOT
A NUMBER OR COLOR

Although we've defined what aging is, it's just as important to define what aging *is not*. Remember that we're not searching for the dictionary definition, we're searching for a marketer's definition. A marketer's definition of aging must reflect the reality of the consumers' behaviors, because in the end it's behavior, not biology, that drives perception and purchase.

To summarize what's been said earlier, age is not about biology, it's about psychology, and the psychology of aging is fundamentally irrational. The rational part of aging – impending mortality – is unpleasant, so people create a more pleasing scenario of aging to compensate. They see aging as the future of living, and they intend to live an uncompromised lifestyle. This is why people continually redefine "old age" as they age, and why they claim to feel younger as they get older. If they're being irrational with age, then the only way we can get better with age is to better understand their irrationality.

If we have a worthy marketer's definition of what aging *is*, why bother defining what aging *is not*? For the simple reason that we learn more from our failures than our successes. As brands begin to experiment with marketing to age, many are still learning as they go, and many are making the same mistakes. They are defining age as a number or a color.

Defining age as a number is an easy trap to fall into because most marketing has always operated in the way media is bought and target audiences are defined. An 18- to 49-year-old audience is the industry standard, and 50+ is that, well, *other* audience. Philosophically and psychologically, it's always been of lesser importance, reflecting the bias that an older consumer is less valuable than a younger one. This internal, ideological belief has a way of manifesting itself in consumer-directed marketing, most often as the dreaded "50+" version we've spoken of elsewhere in the book. Labelling a product by age – or referencing an age in your marketing communications – feels like the right thing to do because, to a rational business mind, it's seen as organizing and defining the brand's offerings in a clear and descriptive way that the consumer can understand. However, when you label your offering by age, you're also labelling the consumer. No one likes to be labelled in general, but especially not when you're overly sensitive to your age. Using numbers is like putting a scarlet letter "O" (for Old) on your package.

It's also best if you avoid using colors like silver or grey in your terminology. Even if it's limited to your internal lexicon, it will find a way to manifest itself externally, despite your best intentions not to.

One of our clients markets a product that helps women with a physical condition brought on by aging. When we were first briefed on the assignment, the women we were being asked to create advertising for were described as "sufferers" – they were seen as suffering from the condition, and therefore needful of our client's product. Without intending to, labelling a woman as a "sufferer" – even if only on internal documents – was influencing the tonality of the communications being created. It was as if our target woman was locked in a struggle with her problem, isolated, depressed, unable to live her life as she wanted for fear of the "serious" condition she was "suffering" from.

We immediately struck this word from the strategy document, and suddenly the whole tenor of the brand's communications began to change. The target woman went from being a "sufferer" to a woman who was celebrated for her positive, joyful, and resilient spirit. The results were profound.

The same is true of color – thinking of the consumer as grey will start you down a path of unintended consequences. Not only is the color grey ubiquitously associated with old age, it's also a color that's dull, bland, and monochromatic. Aging consumers' focus on uncompromised living is anything but dull – they see themselves as vibrant, colorful, and spirited, qualities diametrically opposed to that which is suggested by a color like grey.

Words really matter when it comes to marketing to age, and the words you use internally can often matter as much as those used in consumer-directed communications. Use words your target audience would use, and oh, by the way, these are the people who never talk about their numerical age or the real color of their hair.

BREAK FREE
FROM THE INERTIA
OF SUCCESS

If you always do what you've always done, you'll always get what you've always got. Said another way – if you want change, you'll need to change. One of the biggest challenges in getting better with age is getting over the organizational and personal barriers that impede change, especially when the kind of change we're talking about – marketing to the aging consumer – lacks precedent for most companies. Absent a compelling motivation or dire need to change, attempts to move forward usually succumb to the force of inertia. Inertia holds you in place, a place that makes it easy to do what you've always done because you've done it before, it worked, and it's comfortably familiar.

We'll spare you the clichéd commentary on "getting out of your comfort zone" by sharing a historical analogy from the Gold Rush instead. When word of the gold discovery got out, the prospect for fast riches created a mania that quickly spurred people into action. There was a reason it was called the Gold *Rush*, as speed was of the essence. Those who got to the gold first would discover nuggets on the ground, while those who waited would have to dig deep to find dust. This is the common lore of the Gold Rush, but what has been less historically apparent is that these early prospectors – the original "first movers" – took on enormous risk just to get to the gold, and if they made it that far, they then faced a task with which not a single one of them had one stitch of experience. The absence of a precedent – or "best practice", to use modern parlance – did not deter these courageous men from pursuing gold *because the prospect for wealth was so high*. Simply put, the potential for reward greatly exceeded the perceived risk, and when that happens, action ensues.

While companies talk a lot about managing risk, the actual behavior is one of minimizing risk. Risk has a bad reputation, and with today's imperative to generate predictable results with full accountability, it's not something taken on willingly, *unless* the prospect for reward is irresistibly high.

The best example of this is the emerging market strategy. Companies are willing to take on the risk of doing business in countries where they've never been before because the prospect for easy, fast growth is so high. The prospect for reward is so significant that it distorts the *perception* of risk. There is nothing easy about establishing new businesses in foreign markets, which by definition, are *foreign* – unfamiliar. Yet they have rushed pell-mell to open new markets in far-flung places like Indonesia and South Africa, because each new entrant expects the easy pickings – the proverbial gold nuggets on the ground – and in this zealous state, underestimates the actual risk.

If this thinking is applied to marketing to age, there are fundamentally two ways to break free from the inertia of the status quo: increase perceived reward while decreasing perceived risk. The key word in all of this is *perceived*.

If you have never marketed to age, it's going to be extremely difficult to accurately determine risk and reward. Only by doing do we learn, and absent having done this, you will have little to go on. If you truly want to be a change agent for aging, you will need to think and act like a 49er.

Is there really gold in California?
Will finding gold dramatically change my circumstances?
How and where will I find it?
What happens if I don't?

Aging is a vast, uncontested space; it is the mother lode of marketing. If you succeed, the size of the prize is such that you will have materially advantaged yourself or your company. That was an easy question.

Now what about the other questions? The only way to answer those is to do something. Start moving in the direction of the gold, and trust your instincts and innovative skills to steer you to the source. You'll probably want to take small steps first, but at least you'll be underway, making forward progress with a good chance that your competitors are still searching for a map that doesn't exist and are quickly falling behind.

Again, only by doing do we learn. Test some small, low-risk ideas and you may just get some big learning. As you keep moving and keep learning the new territory of aging, the map will start to fall into place, and each successive step will become more obvious and more productive.

Alas, with movement comes momentum, and it's much harder to stop things once they're rolling. Those personal or organizational barriers that created the inertia of the status quo will not hold up once you start racking up successes.

GET OFF THE
STATIONARY BIKE

Work has become a workout. There's no such thing as going through the motions anymore. You've got to break a sweat every day because if you're not in some pain, there's not going to be a business gain. The markets that we compete in have become overly mature and the speed of innovation poses an ominous competitive threat at every turn.

One strategy for dealing with the heightened demands of work is to work harder. The Boomers know a thing or two about that, because we were born in the day and age of a pronounced work ethic, a remnant of our Depression-era grandparents who worked beyond hard to put food on the table every day. The theory of hard work is pretty basic stuff – the harder you work, the more you will get done, and the faster you will succeed. For years, all you had to do was outwork the guy sitting next to you and you were sure to get the promotion and raise that you wanted.

My, how the times have changed. Nowadays, hard work and being plugged in 24/7 are simply the ante to get in the game, and success comes only to those who can find different ways of doing the same work or working where no one else is. By now, we've established that marketing to age is a juicy opportunity to realize fast growth in an uncontested market space, yet some are still slow to realize this. These are the people who still think work needs to be a workout and who are pedalling away on a stationary bike.

Naturally, a stationary bike doesn't go anywhere. It's an apt metaphor for working really hard at something without moving forward. Chances are, if you're still doing what you've always done – best practices with precedent – you're still pedalling in the same place.

The inertia of marketing to 18- to 49-year-olds is keeping a lot of smart people on their stationary bikes. While they're intelligent enough to know that marketing to age is a chance for some easy pickings, the corporate process (the one that defines ages 18 to 49 as the standard) is instructing them to work hard and stay focused. The culture of the status quo has everyone on a stationary bike doing what they've always done, and the bikers keep pedalling away because they're confusing hard work with progress.

The stationary bike is simply another metaphor in this book, another attempt to put the same message into a more provocative context. None of us wants to work as hard as we are and not have any progress to show for it, so it's time to look around and ask yourself if there is something about your corporate culture and its entrenched definitions of success that may be holding you in place. Inertia is the enemy of progress, and a stationary bike is a pretty sticky image of inertia at its worst.

So if you're still marketing to the 18 to 49 group because that's what you've always done and it's always brought success, perhaps you need to get off the bike and take a nice, cold drink of ice water. You'll find it as refreshing as marketing to age and moving your business forward with every turn.

CROSS THE LINE

A presumption exists in marketing that an older consumer is fundamentally less valuable than a younger consumer. This is bolstered by the belief that as consumers age out of the fashionable 18- to 49-year-old demographic, they cross a line into old age (the forbidden zone of marketing), become set in their ways, spend less money, and rapidly approach senility. Nothing could be further from the truth, and if you want to reap the rewards of doing business in an uncontested market space, you will need to cross the line *with* the aging consumer and *without* the bias of deeply ingrained best practices.

The line of demarcation at age 49 is completely arbitrary, and is the by-product of marketing's obsession with the 18- to 49-year-old target market, which in turn is a by-product of marketing's earlier infatuation with the Baby Boomer generation.

When the first Baby Boomer turned 18 in 1964, and a new generation began searching for the meaning of life, Madison Avenue found meaning in their magnitude. At 80 million strong at the time, they were the mass in mass marketing, and with the advent of electronic media and plastic credit, the modern era of marketing as we know it was born. All the best practices, philosophies, and processes that define marketing to this day are the consequence of courting the

Baby Boomers' coveted loyalty. The most dominant of these best practices was the establishment of the 18- to 49-year-old target audience as the metric on which media was valued.

The industry's inertia around marketing to an 18- to 49-year-old consumer is significant, and difficult to challenge on both philosophical and practical grounds. For as long as marketers believe they need to choose a single, primary target at which to direct their offering, they will choose a consumer aged 18 to 49 for two key reasons. One, it's easier to market to a demographic for which there are familiar best practices and process, and the path of least resistance is always preferred. Two, marketers believe that the comparatively youthful composition of the 18- to 49-year-old cohort represents the future of their businesses. The underlying philosophy here is that if you can win the loyalty of a consumer at a young age, you can retain that loyalty for a lifetime. Hmmm.

This logic is based on the premise of choosing one audience. Doing business is about making decisions, and decisions by nature are about an either-or scenario. However, believing that you need to choose one primary audience is yet another by-product of years of mass marketing to 18- to 49-year-old consumers. With the proliferation of digital media and the ability to create discrete messages for precisely defined and addressable audiences, we no longer live in a world of either-or audience choices – we can now make and-and choices.

To move ahead, you need to leave something behind. If you're going to cross the line to market to the lucrative and numerous consumers who are older than 49, you will need to leave behind the bias that a younger consumer is more valuable than an older one, as well as the mass-marketing philosophy of creating one message for one audience.

The mass inherent in the size of the Baby Boomer generation – now aged 51 to 69 – means that even its subsets are extremely sizeable. If you're going to cross the line, while still valuing the younger consumers on the other side of the line, you will need to segment the Boomer audience.

Typically (here we go again), audiences have been defined by age or stage. Marketers target a consumer based on a definition of age that correlates nicely with the way media is priced and measured, or they market to a stage, eg. a young mother having her first baby.

There is a third model of engagement that will be critical to success. Generational marketing (marketing to a generation's unique set of values and beliefs) taps into personal beliefs and world views. These core values, created during critical formative years, endure for a lifetime, irrespective of age or stage.

With this approach the massive Boomer cohort can be segmented into more discrete audiences that represent the highest potential for your specific offering. For example, if you are a retail bank trying to increase deposit accounts, a values-based segmentation could prioritize audiences that value saving money as part of a predictable and comfortable future, and deprioritize the pleasure-seeking Boomers who are spenders, not savers.

So go ahead and cross the line. The line is completely arbitrary and the prospect of generating fast growth where no one else is doing business is completely objective. What's more, it's fun to break the "rules" every now and then anyway.

SELL UMBRELLAS
WHEN IT RAINS

If you've ever been in Manhattan when it's raining, you've likely witnessed opportunistic salesmanship at its best. The very moment it begins to sprinkle – catching thousands of exposed pedestrians unaware and ill equipped for the coming deluge – out of seemingly nowhere appears the sidewalk umbrella salespeople. No one knows where they come from or how they manage to have their inventory conveniently in place at a moment's notice, but there they are nonetheless, ready to bail you out with a $5 fix. The New York city sidewalk umbrella sellers are truly the original pop-up store.

If you were to write a marketing white paper on the pop-up umbrella seller, the topic would be something like, "Positioning your product at the point of need", and it would focus on classical marketing topics like agility, need states, location, and value.

Agility is used so often these days that it's become a bit of a cliché, but if you're the umbrella seller (we emphasize the first syllable in New York: 'um-brel-la) agility is your raison d'être. Everything about your business model needs to be flexible enough to allow you to respond to a change in meteorological pressure with a retail operation that's up and running in minutes.

Then there are "need states". We talk about them all the time, but usually in a generalized way. We come from a mass-marketing past, so we tend to express need states that are massive and enduring, eg. the consumer wants a cereal high in fiber that also tastes great. If the umbrella seller's marketing team crafted an insight this way, it would read something like: "People use umbrellas because they want to stay dry when it rains." You see the point.

And what about value? The $5 street umbrella is absolutely priceless when the skies open up and you're caught naked only minutes before walking into a big meeting. We're not talking value here, we're talking *invaluable*. That's saying a lot for a product that's so poorly made it's essentially disposable.

Okay, so you're probably saying, "Duh, of course, but I'm not a street vendor, I'm a large multinational brand dealing with all the realities and complexities of scale." Yes, of course, but there's still a very valuable lesson to be learned from our opportunistic umbrella seller.

It's a lesson about the offering and how it's offered.

In a world where technological innovation renders entire categories of products obsolete over night (who needs flashlights, calculators, or clocks when they're on everyone's phone?) the umbrella is one of the simplest, most enduring product designs ever created (think 11th century China). Hard to believe, but true.

The umbrella is an example of timeless innovation because of its brutal simplicity. Don't let technology complicate what you create simply because it's available to you. Tivoli Audio – "The Original Radio Company" – theoretically has no reason for being in today's digitally dominated world of sound, but regardless, it's thriving. Why? The company did some basic research and learned that digital technology had gone too far. Valuable consumers like the Boomers were asking for simple, intuitive table radios with knobs and dials in lieu of touch screens. They figured out that success in radios is about touch, not sound; they replaced high-tech with high-touch.

The umbrella guy's marketing plan doesn't stop with his brilliant offering – he's built a business model that ensures that it's offered at precisely the time that it's needed most. In Economics 101 terms, he's way out there on the supply-demand curve because he's been able to efficiently supply his product when demand is high. Precision like this multiplies the value of the offering, which is why something "cheap" like the street umbrella is deemed to be "priceless."

The real moral to this quaint story is that you can't let your scale obscure opportunism. No matter how big and successful your business is, you have to be sure that you understand what's going on at the street level. Do you really know your core consumer and do you truly understand the dynamics of their needs? Our Manhattan executive who's dashing to a meeting in the rain has an acute need at a point in time that makes a $5 umbrella priceless. If you're working with consumer understanding that's as blunt as, "People want a quality umbrella that will keep them dry," then watch out – some sharp guy down the street might just put you out of business.

DO IT
WITH FEELING

I f you're creating advertising for aging consumers, it's imperative that your message makes them feel something. While it's also important to have them *think* differently about your product, it will be insufficient if it fails to engender feeling.

The original definition of advertising – prior to the advent of electronic media – was "salesmanship in print". That definition is so pithy and provocative – even after all these years – that it's almost an ad in and of itself. It's easy to get and it's easy to buy into.

Despite that, the essence of advertising still eludes many marketers, even the witty folks who make it. One of the great tendencies of Madison Avenue is to get overly obsessed with the craft and creativity of advertising, so much so that they're prone to lose track of what the advertising they're creating is supposed to do. At its most fundamental level, its purpose is to sell something by getting someone to buy it. In the day and age of return on investment (ROI) and heightened accountability, you now need to sell enough of what you're selling to pay for the cost of the advertising, and then some. If you think "salesmanship in print" is getting harder by the day, try creating it for an aging consumer.

Aging consumers are different than typical consumers, which means you'll need to do things differently to be effective. For starters, neuroscience has revealed that their cognitive and reasoning processes are slower, and that they prefer to process information presented in a linear or narrative format. They also rely more on their intuition and instincts – emotionally driven traits – which means they are more apt to respond to things that feel right on a "gut" level.

If your advertising approach is one of "selling by telling", you're likely to come up short. You'll need more than that to appeal to the emotional way in which the aging consumer will process your message.

Instead of telling, you'll want to consider storytelling. Stories are narrative by nature and they engage by appealing to the emotionally dominant part of the brain. There is psychology to storytelling. As author Philip Pullman (novelist) once said: "After nourishment, shelter, and companionship, stories are the thing we need most in the world." When told well, there is nothing more captivating than a story. There are many theories as to why stories work, but as they pertain to the aging consumer, the key influences are a story's ability to offer messages or morals that resonate with the consumer's own life experiences, wrapped up in imagery that's positive and aspirational.

Aging consumers are optimistic and intend to lead a long life characterized by wellbeing, joy, and growth. If these are the ambitions that they're most passionate about, they will naturally choose to relate to those brands and messages that mirror their own self-image.

While all of this seems straightforward, large categories of advertisers have struggled to optimize their message to the aging consumer, notably the financial services companies that pitch retirement products.

For many financial services brands, the norm is "selling by telling" and the telling part often borders on the negative. A Boomer doesn't need to be told that they haven't saved enough for retirement or that they may outlive their savings. On a rational level, they already know that – instead, they are irrationally choosing to ignore the facts because their optimistic nature has them imagining a more aspirational future.

Give them credit – these brands are trying to evoke a powerful emotion, but it's a negative one: fear. The use of negative emotion is always a slippery slope, but when it's used for an aging consumer who is embracing positivity and optimism to offset the negative consequences of aging, it can be a quick slide down the mountain.

No one can summarize this better than Maya Angelou once did: "I've learned that people will forget what you said, people will forget what you did, but people will never forget how you made them feel."

If you're going to target aging consumers, be sure to create a story that exudes positive emotion, and if you tell it with feeling, they'll likely remember how you made them feel. When you do things with feeling, you create a connection that makes a lasting impression.

BEWARE OF
THE GENERATIONAL
ABYSS

The numbers don't lie … and the future they portend is not a pretty one. Despite our industry's zealous devotion to Millennials, the fact is that marketers won't be able to count on them to become the kind of mature, sophisticated, high-volume consumers that their Boomer parents have been until about 2030 … at the earliest. Many marketers will be facing a daunting generational transition for the next 15 years.

As part of my commitment to the aging consumer, I'm frequently invited to speak to gatherings of influential people across a great diversity of businesses – from financial services to fashion to luxury goods and more. In the past two years, these sessions have often taken the form of a "debate", or more accurately a "staged confrontation" between Boomers and Millennials. Marketers are thinking either-or and they want to know which generation is more valuable.

What most audiences discover – often to their great puzzlement and sometimes to their delight – is that Boomers and Millennials actually have more in common than not. If you look beyond their behavioral peccadillos, you'll discover that they actually share a core set of values, particularly around their sense of individuality and experiential orientations. This is not surprising when you remember that the Millennials are, by and large, the children of Boomers.

Arguably, no two generations in modern history have been more emotionally and culturally connected.

The fundamental challenge that most marketers seem to be debating is whether to prioritize the Millennials ("the future of my franchise") or the Boomers ("my brand loyalists who are getting older"). Here's what most of them know ... and *don't* know. They know that Baby Boomers – the Most Valuable Generation™ of nearly 76 million rabid consumers who powered the US and global economy from the end of WWII to the end of the 20th century – have given way to a new generation: Millennials – just as large, and destined to propel economic growth and human achievement to even more stratospheric heights. This highly educated, digital-media-savvy cohort will one day "rule" global society and the consumer marketing culture just as their parents once did.

While it's clear that Millennials represent the future for brands and businesses, it's far less clear when that future will arrive. Marketers are staring at the clock ... but it has no hands.

Consider that the current age range of the Millennials is 20 to 38, with the bulk of them in the middle of a demographic "bell curve". Add to that what we know about when people marry, have families, and build households, and then factor in the college debt burdens and depressed pay scales for most jobs that have postponed these decisions for Millennials. You quickly come to the inescapable conclusion that the leading edge of Millennials will not achieve the spending power of their Boomer parents for another five years ... and most of the rest not until 2030. If you're in categories such as big-ticket durables or luxury goods, you're staring at a 15-year abyss before Millennials make the full generational transition.

The only positive spin, if there is one, is that "late-blooming" Millennials – who are more likely to stay in the job market longer and have fewer children than their parents – will help to readjust the projected imbalance between inflows and outflows in the Social Security trust fund. This means that it may not be in danger of defaulting on its obligation to the Boomers as they continue to retire at the blistering pace of 10,000 per day for the next 15 years.

As with every other life stage, Boomers are redefining "aging" and "retirement" unlike any generation in history. They are staying healthier, more active, more relevant, and more connected than previous generations; and they still control more discretionary income and luxury-goods spending than any other consumer cohort.

Those Boomers who do "retire" are becoming *more* active, not less. They're renovating, traveling, volunteering, starting new businesses, celebrating anniversaries, getting remarried, and also taking a more active role in the lives of their children – and grandchildren.

So if you're one of those marketers who are staring out into the distance trying to figure out what the future looks like, you might want to look down instead. Depending on what business you're in, there's a good chance that there's a gaping generational gap right at your feet. It's quite possible that it's going to be another 15 years before the generational bridge is complete, and if that's the case, you're going to need a new plan. It's time to turn around and focus on the valuable consumers you already have. Remember, the Boomers are big, valuable, and they love the brands that love them. If you continue to embrace them, you're sure to keep your business on solid ground for years to come.

TAKE SOME
FLYING LESSONS

I f you're going to take on the challenge of marketing to age – to perhaps go where you're organization has never been before – you're going to need have "the right stuff". Naturally, you will need resources and the commitment of your company, but you will also need to approach the opportunity with a suitable level of coolness, courage, and fearlessness to take on a challenge that poses a not insignificant level of risk. But if you approach risk with the right attitude and confidence, you will surely succeed and with that will come meaningful business reward and perhaps even a tad of personal glory.

Tom Wolfe coined the phrase "right stuff" in his eponymously named movie featuring the intensely intrepid test pilot, Chuck Yeager. While marketing is not as perilous as high-speed flight, it may feel that way at times if you're taking risks within a conservative corporate culture. The reason that dauntless people like Yeager can repeatedly expose themselves to excessive risk and prevail is that they've been trained properly – they've been conditioned to risk and have an uncanny ability to do the right thing when things go wrong.

The Air Force has a philosophical approach to this scenario summed up as, "Plan the flight and then fly the plan ... but don't fall in love with the plan." Most corporate cultures embrace and execute the first two aspects of this advice – plan the work and work the plan – but they usually lack the ability to successfully course correct when the plan encounters an unexpected obstacle. In this case, they lack "the right stuff" in the form of the ability to instinctively react in the moment. This is typically because the risk-reward culture of their organization discourages instinctual behavior because it is individualistic. Instead, they prefer to believe that the vast resources and experience of their collective organization are better suited to address the situation than the acts of one person. Said another way, the company wants to believe that it has the right stuff to help you in the time of need.

There are two issues with what I've just described. First, the most innovative and successful companies have found ways to inspire their intrepid people to act as individuals when circumstances require agility and responsiveness. They do so because they're smart enough to know that all of the resources and wherewithal of the broader organization are irrelevant if they cannot be leveraged at the moment of need. It doesn't matter how capable the fire engine is if the fire-fighters can't get it to the fire on time.

Second, they've ignored the third component of the Air Force's wisdom, "Don't fall in love with the plan." Given that the Air Force is in constant contact with danger, it's seen more brilliant plans fail than most, while also witnessing the ability of highly capable and well-trained individuals to vs. yo react immediately to get a new plan in place. In more cases than not, these individuals don't have a support network to back them up, and since pulling the eject handle can often be lethal, they figure it out "on the fly".

As you start to market to age, there's a reasonably good chance that your initial plan is going to go out the window. If you've prepared yourself for that eventuality – by preventing yourself from blindly falling in love with the going-in plan – you'll be anticipating a hitch and be at the ready to course correct appropriately with a new plan of action. Said another way, you'll be prepared to be prepared. Above all else, if you've decided that there is compelling value in prioritizing the aging consumer, you will need to demonstrate commitment, the willingness to stay the course, and to persevere as the dynamics of the aging marketplace change as inevitably as age itself. If you can truly commit yourself to go where no one else yet has, you will create your own wind under your wings and you will soar, and when you do, you're going to go places, fast.

LOOK FOR THE
RED FLAGS THAT
YOU CAN'T SEE

O n my way to fish in a remote section of Labrador, we had a layover in Labrador City. As I left the airport building and hopped into a waiting taxi, I noticed something that I had never seen before. Virtually every car had a nine-foot tall fluorescent red flag attached to its rear bumper. Seeing my puzzled expression, the taxi driver explained that these were warning flags. Unbeknownst to me, Labrador City is home to a major strip mining operation and the mine's massive goliath trucks share the same roads with the town's automobiles. Given the towering height of these mining trucks, their drivers are positioned too high above the road surface to see normal sized vehicles on the road below. The cars are in the trucks' vertical blind spots and their highflying red flags serve to alert the trucks to their presence.

If you are a senior leader at a large company operating in a massive category, you're a lot like a Labrador City mine truck driver. Because of your elevated position in the company, you will fundamentally have blind spots when it comes to recognizing what's going on below you and/or around you. Inside the company, you're likely to have people who are operating in these blind spots without an obligation to alert you of their activities. Externally, there are areas of your competitive landscape that are also invisible, either because you're looking in the wrong direction or because your competitors have kept them secret. The mine truck driver has a major advantage that you don't – his blind spots wave red flags at him to capture his attention.

Since the blind spots in your business are by definition blind, they're obviously not going to alert you to their presence. Instead, you will need to improve your vision to be able to see things you couldn't see before. To do this, you will need to understand that your vision is correlated to your vantage point i.e. where you are positioned determines your line of sight which in turn influences your perception of things. Think of the image of train tracks extending to the horizon – they create an optical illusion of converging in the distance. Only by moving your position – walking toward the distant horizon where the tracks seemingly narrow – do you discover that the tracks are actually still parallel; your original vantage point had been misleading and you only discover reality when you look at things differently.

To be a leader who truly has a full vision of your business, you will constantly need to change your vantage point to ensure that you are seeing all aspects of your business from different perspectives. We often use phrases like "seeing things in a different light" or "looking at things from a different angle" without realizing that we are actually talking about the discovery of our blind spots. When we see things differently, we spot the red flags.

We also know that arrogance is blinding, and the arrogance that we see most often in business is the over-confidence that results in complacency. These are the companies that are blind to a new or different way of doing things because they are only looking in the direction of the things they've always done. A great example of this is the taxi and limousine industry, dominating one day only to be pushed toward extinction by Uber's technologically inspired ridership concept. It's remarkable to think that a market force of this magnitude and potency could be hiding in a blind spot of such a significant industry. Everyone in business has an Uber in their blind spot – the issue is that they just can't see it yet.

The economic value of the aging market dwarfs a business like Uber, yet because most marketers have their sights fixated on an 18-49 consumer, it too is in a blind spot. One by one, the Boomers are starting to raise their red flags to let marketers now that they're still here, still spending, but starting to feel ignored. They're looking to get your attention and if you fail to notice, one of two things is going to happen: they'll either drive their business to another brand or they'll be spotted by that brand before they appear on your radar. With so much at stake, this is an obvious example of the need to look for the red flags that you can't see. It's time to be a different kind of "visionary."

HELP THEM
REIMAGINE

The Boomers will be reaching retirement age at the rate of 10,000 a day for the next 15 years, but most won't be retiring. Instead, they'll simply be pausing to reimagine their lives so they can hit the reset button and get on to what's next. Given that marketing is particularly effective when it targets "apertures" – significant changes in consumers' lives that open their minds to new possibilities – it's important to be ready to become an essential part of their new life experiences.

In a 2013 study conducted by Merrill Lynch and Age Wave, 70% of pre-retirees indicated that they planned to continue working after "retiring" from their current jobs. A percentage as significant as this is clearly driven by a passion to stay engaged, but also a need to generate income.

Given that so many Boomers will be looking for jobs that either don't exist or don't fit their skills, many will need to reimagine themselves in the role of small business owners. As such, we are about to witness one of the most pronounced periods of entrepreneurialism that our country has ever seen, which is a massive aperture for brands that can support aging workers' new dreams.

Let's say you're a local retail bank looking to grow deposits and revenue. You might consider targeting Millennials, but it's well established that this generation is challenged on both sides of the ledger with outstanding college debt and low job income that's commensurate with their age. What's more, they don't yet have a thorough grasp of financial matters, and those that do bank actively are more inclined to use digital products versus having a bricks-and-mortar branch relationship.

Enter the Boomers. Not only do they control a dominating percentage of our country's disposable income, but they also have a mature grasp of finances and longstanding bank relationships. Now scads of them will look to start their own businesses, many of them for the first time. They will lack capital and foundational small business know-how and will be all too eager to welcome help from their local bank, *if* that bank was smart enough to create a new suite of products and services custom-created to help the Boomers navigate this new phase of their life.

Similarly, as the Boomers leave the traditional workplace and start spending their days in their homes, they will likely want to or need to transform their homes to accommodate their new life and work styles. Businesses like big box home improvement or office supply stores should want to get way out in front of this trend.

In change there is opportunity. This is the fundamental tenet that makes aperture marketing so brilliantly effective, but it doesn't stop there. What's equally noteworthy is the fact that consumers usually don't forget how you helped them or made them feel at the point in time when their need was most dire.

The transition from years and years of traditional employment to an entrepreneurial endeavor will not be without stress and growing pains. Just imagine how powerful it could be if your brand was right where it needed to be at their time of need – not only would you sell a lot of product, you would also generate a lifetime of goodwill for being more than just a purveyor, but for being an essential partner in the right place at the right time.

An opportunity like this is unprecedented in its magnitude. The Most Valuable Generation™ in the history of marketing is living one of the most dramatic changes in a long lifetime. Those brands and businesses that are the most imaginative will benefit the most from serving a generation that is being imaginative about the rest of their lives. Think beyond what you think is possible because this is the generation that believes anything is possible.

THE SECRET TO SUCCESS IS KNOWING THE SECRETS

B y virtue of the fact that you're reading this book, there's a pretty good chance that you're a person who's motivated to succeed. You're committed to continuous learning because you know that the right piece of knowledge or insight – leveraged to its fullest – can lead to a potent competitive advantage. All of us are driven to succeed in some way, but what ultimately sets us apart is the amount of innate talent we start with, combined with the amount of effort we are willing to invest in building those skills or acquiring new ones. If you intend to market to age, it's time to get to work to figure out how you're going to win. As you do so, you will have many options to explore, but the surest path to success is to determine a way to figure out the secrets that your competitors have not yet deciphered.

Let's start at the starting point. Most of us work as part of broader company teams. The path to success at many large agencies or marketing organizations is a trans-functional process. Each member of the team is dependent on the unique skills that other members contribute, and we commit ourselves to working as interdependently as possible. We usually have ambitious expectations and aggressive timelines, so we dive right into the work at hand, and if everything goes as planned, there's a pretty good chance we'll succeed.

Earlier in my career, I hired a team-building specialist to help our agency team with a particularly challenging client dynamic. I had planned for the training to take place offsite, which was met with the usual grumbling and cynicism that comes with asking over-worked people to spend time they don't have doing something they don't believe in. To them, this was a "nice to do", not a "need to do". After all, we had all managed our way through difficult client dynamics before – and surely would again – so why the need for new religion and more time away from home?

None of them would ever forget how the training started. After exchanging the obligatory pleasantries, we were all asked to name some of the most successful teams we knew. Most people named professional sports teams, and when our trainer prodded us to think outside of sports, some volunteered teams like symphony orchestras or ballet troupes. When we were then asked what all of these highly successful teams had in common, the desired answer eluded all of us. It was at that point that the epiphany of all of my years of teamwork was branded on my forehead: the best teams in the world practice more than they perform. Obvious, yet surprising.

Here we were, working for one of the most accomplished ad agencies in the world, and we were absolutely convinced that we were so good that we didn't need to practice. Pity those professional teams that need to practice so much. Not us – we were so good that we were going to knock it out of the park every time.

The point of this story is that if you want to win consistently – which is what top-performing teams do – you will need to do more than just show up to play and will successful outcomes. You need a plan – something more than just resources, hard work, and good intent. Said another way, you'll need a plan to figure out the secrets to success.

A symphony orchestra's secret to success is a three-act affair: hire the best performers available, add a conductor who can bring out their best work, and follow with practice, practice, and more practice. Since most of us don't work in cultures that encourage practice (we're too busy – heck, who has the time to practice?), the only way we are going to come close to replicating it is by tapping the skills of highly experienced people, people who have been *practicing* the trade for years.

Which brings us back to knowing the secrets of success. By definition, people with more experience will have discovered more of the secrets than the newcomers. To market to age, it is almost a mandate that your team consists of some people who have lived the lives of aging consumers. If so, they will be contributing at least two essential skills: as people of age, their career experience will be extensive, and secondly, they are living the lives of the consumers whose lives you are trying to improve.

Once you've added some "people with secrets" to your team, you'll want to continue your quest for the secrets to success. In doing so, you'll want to consider the following "clues".

To find them, you will need to look for them. Obvious? Not really. In many tasks of life, we are so focused on the act of completing the work at hand that we seldom take the time to observe the *way* things are being done. If we're simply looking to get things done, we will miss out on the nuances of the process, the subtle little things that can often be the difference between success and failure.

Another way to get at the secrets of success is to be more inquisitive about *how* things work. Over the course of a long career in advertising, I have worked with many people capable of creating advertising that works but who can't really explain *why* it works. Advertising is a refined art of sales, and any good salesperson can go on at length about the art of making the sale. When advertising folks are asked to explain the difference between good work and great work, they point to great work, but they're missing the point. It's not *what* it is; the secret is to know *how* it works. What's more, when you know how something works, there's a pretty good chance that you'll also know how to fix it when it's broken.

Lastly, contrary to the general rule of thumb, don't keep your secrets a secret. Once you put your finger on something that is going to give you a competitive advantage, make sure the right people on your team are also aware. A great secret is too good not to be shared.

HAVE AN INSIGHT
FOR INSIGHTS

usiness loves jargon and acronyms. As marketers, we have a language of our own, replete with buzzwords and catchphrases that help to keep us living at the cutting edge of the newest new. Oddly, most of our favorite vocabulary consists of words that start with the letter "I". Think about it. How often do you use terms like issue, information, intelligence, impressions, insight, inspiration, ideas, and of course, integration? I call it the "I (eye) Chart" of marketing.

While some of these will come and go over time, insights and ideas will remain eternally core to what we do in marketing and especially communications. If I had my way, we would drastically simplify our language and our process so we could focus on what matters most in the end: discovering the insights that inspire great ideas. But if insights are what sparks growth, and great insights are hard to find, why don't we have insights to help us find better insights? It's not unlike another catchphrase that we love – planning the plan.

Let's face it, really great insights are hard to find. I once had a client who quipped that the best insights were not only hard to find, they actually hide from you. Trust me, there have been many times when I was convinced that the insights I was seeking were running the other way. Once you find one, you'll know it's brilliant if it surprises you with its obviousness.

As Galileo once said, "All truths are easy to understand once they are discovered. The point is to discover them."

Here are two insights for getting better insights that are hopefully surprising yet easy to understand. The first is the observation that to unearth better insights, you need to dig in the right place. Its obviousness has to do with the fact that most marketers tend to dig in the most obvious aspects of the category experience. They ask, "How do my consumers use my products, what do they yearn for that my current offering doesn't deliver, and how are my competitors stacking up relative to consumer expectations?" Despite all of the advances in marketing understanding and analytics, most marketers and agencies are still content to seek out insights using the traditional Venn-Diagram approach – what do we know to be true about the brand, what do we know to be true about the consumer, and the point at which they overlap is where you will find the insight. X marks the spot? Guess what. It's not that easy.

It's been my experience that the best insights are usually found in the less obvious places, where no one else has looked. You will have to get off the proverbial "beaten path" to dig in areas that have not yet seen a shovel. In most instances, these rich areas are the seams or edges adjacent to the obvious spots. We have had great success with the aging consumer by avoiding the temptation to look for insights in the obvious area of symptomology. It's less about what your product or service can do to solve the issues or problems associated with age and more about what it can do to address aging consumers' feelings about the issue, which in turn have more to do with their feelings about aging.

The second insight on insights is that sometimes you're not actually looking for insights; you're simply looking to interpret the intelligence you already have in a different way. In this regard, interpretation is the most important "I" word that's not a part of our everyday marketing vocabulary.

Many of our client organizations have CI departments, as in Consumer Insights. An interesting way to think differently about this important function is that while CI's goal is to find great insights, the way they do that is to *interpret* what they learn in a way that makes the revelation surprisingly obvious. Done the right way, the I in CI stands for interpretation and the function is staffed with interpreters, not researchers or strategists. As discussed elsewhere in this section of the book, the ability to interpret requires that you speak the consumer's language. True consumer understanding (the path to insights) necessitates that you listen to what they're saying, and translate their words to reveal their true meaning. When aging consumers say they feel in control of their health, what they really mean is that they've come to terms with their loss of control. They can still benefit from your help, especially if you help validate their confidence about their future wellbeing.

Assuming you've managed to dig in the right place and found a way to interpret what you've learned accurately, you will still not have succeeded at finding a great insight until that insight proves that it can lead to a great idea. All too often, the insight process ends when the words are crafted and added to the appropriate box on the strategy document, but it's really just the beginning. Great insights are great because they also *inspire* great ideas. They inspire great ideas because the insights are so compelling that they motivate the people creating the ideas. The insight needs to arouse creative minds and excite them with what's possible, and let's remember, creative minds respond best when the challenge is simple. Virtually any great campaign is based on a simple idea that's memorable. They're simple because they were powered by an equally as brutal, simple insight. Creativity begins where it begins and that's with insights, specifically how and where you look for them. Now that's insightful.

LIVE THE GOLDEN RULE OF MARKETING TO AGE: THERE IS NO SILVER BULLET

While we live in a digital world where customized messages can be addressed to discrete audiences, the enduring philosophies and practices of mass marketing still color much of our thinking. We still want to create that one message that will resonate with all people – the proverbial silver bullet. If only it was that easy.

Why do we look for silver bullets? It's human nature and it's a mass marketing best practice. First, the human part. How many times have you found yourself trying to diagnose a personal or professional dilemma, trying to find *the* explanation as to why things aren't the way you want them to be?

Let's suppose that a member of your team has been acting out of character recently and negatively affecting the team's spirit and performance. You're perplexed, you want an explanation, so you start to have a conversation with yourself: "Why is Charlie behaving this way? Did something happen? Is it an ego or control thing? Is he frustrated or annoyed? Is he lashing out and trying to make a statement?" On and on you go in pursuit of the explanation, which often eludes you because you are looking for *the* explanation, the single answer that sums up Charlie's behavior in a neat and tidy nutshell. The reality is that most of human behavior is not that simple

– in truth, it's actually quite complex. The reason you might fail to understand Charlie's conduct is because you were searching for *an* answer when there were actually several. You were looking at his behavior the wrong way because it's our tendency to simplify – simple is easier.

From a marketing standpoint, we also have a bias to search for silver bullets because we bring our human tendencies to work with us (see the example above) and because the fundamental premise of mass marketing is to identify one target audience and deliver one message to a mass audience with maximum efficiency. The entire creative development and validation process – which can take months and even years – is focused on identifying that one message that most people will find most motivating. That's been the model because that's what's worked for all of these years, beginning in 1964 when the first of the then 80 million US Baby Boomers turned 18, entered the 18- to 49-age cohort and became the literal "mass" in mass marketing.

If you're marketing to the aging consumer, the silver-bullet approach is probably not going to be practical. Unless you've got a really mainstream innovation and a sizeable investment to match, you'll likely be unable to afford a mass approach to a generation that's as massive as the Boomers. Further, many brands are prioritizing younger generations with a secondary emphasis on those aged 49+. If so, it's nearly impossible to balance both targets at a mass delivery funding level.

Instead, you will need to segment the aging audience to identify the subsets of consumers with the highest potential vis-à-vis your offering. With the proliferation of digital technology and media, we now have access to incredibly deep, insightful analytics. This finite intelligence can help us predict behavior and deliver specific messages programmatically so they are consumed at that point in time and place where an aging consumer is most likely to be receptive to your message. In this context, messages can be customized to specific cohorts of consumers based on their known needs and tendencies. We are moving from a model of mass marketing to one of mass customization.

Naturally, a customized message will resonate more effectively than a generic one, but this is likely to be even more pronounced with an aging consumer. As noted earlier in the book, the Boomers have always valued personalization and customization, having come of age as a generation that the world catered to because their size commanded responsiveness.

All of this is to say that when it comes to marketing to a cohort as large and as valuable as the aging consumer, one must shift the emphasis from looking for commonalities to searching for differences – differences between consumers and their unique needs, preferences, and tendencies, and differences in the way you do things. After all, if you want to do things differently, you'll have to work differently and that means finding gold by resisting silver-bullet thinking.

SPEAK THEIR
LANGUAGE –
WORDS MATTER

A s Galileo once said, "All truths are easy to understand once they are discovered; the point is to discover them." It seems as though even a scientist can have a way with words, as his message is as clear as a night sky: the obvious is not always obvious.

Speaking the consumer's language is an obvious requirement of all marketing communication. It's as basic as it gets – seek first to be understood, then strive to persuade. If this is so obvious, why is it that so much of the communication created for aging consumers fails at the most fundamental level? Too much of it simply doesn't speak their language and thus ceases to persuade.

The communication fails to speak to them because the people writing it aren't fluent in the language of the aging consumer. The average age of an advertising agency employee is 27. It's hard to blame them for not speaking the language of someone who is living a life that they themselves are several decades away from experiencing. Even the best training in the world would be insufficient. To see the world the way the aging consumer sees it, you need to experience it the way they have experienced it.

This disconnect with the aging consumer takes many forms, but the most prevalent "mis-translation" is the use of numbers to describe aging. Earlier in the book, aging was defined as "the future of living". In this way, aging is a forward-moving dynamic that represents growth and opportunity and reflects the joy that comes with age. Aging is all of these things and more, but it is not a number.

All too often, marketers label a line extension as a "50+ formula". The logic is that the age designation will differentiate the new product from the brand's other products, while also proudly proclaiming that they have a product that's especially for older people like you.

Not only does this approach fail to be effective, it runs the risk of offending. Old people don't want to be told that they're old, and a number like 50+ might as well be a scarlet letter – it stigmatizes and alienates.

Another miscue is to speak to their problems, as a way to pitch one's product as the solution. This is a timeless, and quite effective format, known in advertising parlance as "problem-solution".

It's a go-to approach for many consumer packaged goods (CPG) brands, and generally works in most product categories and consumer cohorts, until you get to the aging consumer. With these folks, the problem with problem-solution advertising is the problem itself

When the drama of your communication focuses on the problem that the product solves, you're telling aging consumers that they're broken and need to be fixed. Naturally, consumers know they've changed with age and that some things just don't work the way they used to, but they don't want an advertiser to remind them of it or to trade on their age-related ailments.

Instead, they are taking on aging as it comes, with a positive and resilient spirit. They refuse to be defined or reduced by the consequences of aging, so they are looking for those brands and products that "speak their language". Who are you to talk to them about their problems? What they want instead is your help, your understanding, and perhaps a little empathy. Obvious, right?

Lastly, there is power in words, and a few of them used in the right way can have a potent effect – used incorrectly, they can be toxic. Think of this as the pronunciation part of speaking a language. You may be using all of the right words, but if they are not pronounced the right way, you will not be understood. When you fail first to be understood, you will always fail to persuade.

Language is important and the only language that matters is the language of the consumer you are talking to. You can either become fluent – hard to do and time consuming – or you can use a translator. Find the people in your organization already fluent in the language of the aging consumer – they will be the ones who are living the same life as your consumer, 24/7.

Once you achieve this fluency, something beautiful will happen. The consumer you value most will fully embrace your brand because you've done the most obvious but most effective thing in marketing. By speaking their language, you will have demonstrated that you understand them. Nothing is more motivating than to be understood, because it demonstrates that you respect them enough to care about them.

GET AHEAD BY GETTING STARTED

T he reason they called it the Gold Rush was because speed was of the essence. Those who got to California first struck it rich, quickly. Speed is as relevant today as it was then, and fast growth has replaced sustained growth as the new business imperative. But alas, speed is not achievable unless you are first set in motion.

Fast growth is the reward for those who move first. These are the people who have the courage to go where others have not gone for the opportunity to do business where no one else has. First movers, by the very definition of the term, are those who move – they have started with the goal of getting ahead.

For first movers to achieve their advantage, they have to either move faster than others are moving or be moving when no one else is. Given that marketing to age is still an emerging market, most of you will have the advantage of moving when others are not.

What holds people back? Inertia, comfort, and fear.

Inertia is a powerful force that holds things at rest. In most organizations, it is the consequence of well-entrenched philosophies about the way things should be done. It's the result of prior successes and best practices that perpetuate a tendency to do things the way they've always been done because they've always worked.

Inertia also creates complacency because it holds people in a particular place that we've come to call a comfort "zone". You can hardly blame folks, as it's human nature to seek comfort, especially if you work in an organization that makes you fearful of failure.

How do you break free? You take the first step.

Simple and logical, but not really. Most people don't take the first step in the direction of change because a step in an unfamiliar direction has the tendency to feel like a leap. Instead, we "look before we leap" and because a leap feels scary, we do nothing. We end up paralyzed in place, and take not so much as a small step.

The 49ers who moved first to get the gold took a massive leap of faith when they headed west. The risk that was inherent in that leap was okay because the prospect of success was so compelling. In modern parlance, the reward was seen as far outweighing the risk.

If your organization has determined that marketing to age has the potential to be enormously lucrative, the prospect of success will generate its own momentum. You won't be thinking about steps or leaps because you'll be too busy moving.

If not, you will need to break free from the inertia of the status quo by forcing yourself to take small steps. It's like anything else in life – once you get a little bit of experience, that which once seemed impossible is suddenly a walk in the park.

To take that first step, you will need to adjust the risk-reward trade-off that's likely getting in the way. When the risk of an endeavor is perceived as being greater than the reward, you're stuck staring at a red light.

The easiest way to get to a green light is to rethink the scale of the endeavor that in turn rebalances the underlying risk-reward equation. It's amazing how quickly projects can get approved when they're billed as, "Make a little, sell a little." Hey, what's the worst thing that could happen?

The point of all of this is that marketing to age is a change agenda – change involves risk and risk is bad. The way around this, and hence the way forward, is to redefine risk, not as the peril in doing something differently but as the peril inherent in doing nothing at all. Risk is the money lost in a missed opportunity.

The potential in marketing to the uncontested aging space is the obvious opportunity at hand. The first movers are already on the move, but there's still time to act quickly to realize the fast growth in aging. As you ponder what's next, seek inspiration from an ancient Chinese proverb: "Even the longest of journeys begins with a single step." It's time to get started.

SEE THE WORLD
THE WAY THEY SEE IT

T he Rashoman Quandry, a term derived from Akira Kurosawa's period drama film, reminds us that we can only understand how people behave if we have seen the world the way they have. Because most marketers lack the life experience of older consumers, they lack the ability to deeply relate to their lives in the meaningful way that effective marketing requires.

There are two messages here. The first is that you need to be willing to admit what you don't know. It's hardly your fault that you're not the same age with the same life experience as the aging consumer. But *it* is your fault if you forge ahead blindly believing that you are smart enough to understand a very iconoclastic consumer, or that you can blow bluntly crafted messages past the most experienced and savviest of consumers.

The second message is that you will need a new pair of glasses to help you see aging consumers' lives the way they see it. You don't need to have all the answers, you simply need to know where to find answers.

If you want to learn more about how a lion hunts, you wouldn't go to the zoo, you would go to the jungle. To see the world the way aging consumers see it, you need to spend time with them, live in their lives. It's easier to go to the zoo, and in so doing, you might be able to convince yourself that you learned something you didn't know about lions, but if success lies in understanding the hunt, you will have looked for answers in the wrong place.

We recently did some work with a major detergent brand that was trying to better understand the habits and practices of the aging consumer. The prevailing belief was that aging empty nesters were blissfully enjoying being liberated from the toil of endless loads of family laundry, and were content to run fewer wash loads – a good reason to not prioritize them. When we went into their homes and spent time doing laundry with them, we learned something altogether different.

The aging consumer misses the daily task of doing laundry because it's one of the key activities that she associates with the prime of her life when she was the proud caretaker of an active household. A task that had once been physical – think one monotonous load of laundry after another without reward – was now emotional. Doing the laundry is something she now looks forward to. It is a source of joy because it emotionally validates her self-image as a provider. Further, we learned that the process of converting dirty clothing into clean clothing is restorative. There is emotional power in transforming things into a better state – rejuvenating them – which really resonates with an aging consumer who values vitality in all things.

By putting ourselves in her life – if even just for a few hours – we were able to see her life the way she sees it, not the way we see it.

An aging consumer about to be written out of the script was now seen in a heroic role as a highly valuable consumer who brought the power of emotion to a category presumed to be physical.

The lesson here is that the eye only sees what the mind is prepared to comprehend. Said another way, there's no way to know what you don't know. If you are willing to see things you've never seen before – by living the life of the aging consumer – your mind will comprehend and great ideas will follow.

REVELATION,
NOT REVOLUTION

B
ig business has grand expectations. It's not enough to simply grow anymore; now we're being urged to transform our brands, or to *revolutionize* how we do business. On the one hand, this is a great way to rally the troops, to inspire them with a glorious vision that will bring a splendid victory while vanquishing the competition forever. On the other hand, the raising of the bar in this way runs the risk of stretching the organization beyond the boundaries of its capabilities and inflicting defeat from within.

While the way that we talk about marketing to age has all of the business potential associated with aggressive intent like transformation, we prefer to think of it as a revelation not a revolution. We are looking to enlighten, to shine the light on a new way to embrace the aging consumer; to do so, we need not overthrow the status quo of marketing to 18- to 49-year-olds, we simply need to illuminate something new and different to let you decide if it's better.

We've all been at that company meeting where someone stands in the pulpit and evangelizes like a zealot to implore us to take the journey to the Promised Land. For some, it stirs the soul and for others who have been down this road before, it strikes fear in the heart. How many times have you been asked to support the "new agenda" only to find out that it was the wrong agenda once some new leader comes along with another new agenda? It's dizzying, and it's not enjoyable to run a business when you're running away from the new direction.

Marketing to age is not a new "agenda" in that there's no motive behind it other than the compelling opportunity to do business where no one else is. You need not listen to a preacher in a pulpit because the evidence speaks for itself. You need not read the *Bible* or sing from the hymnal because it's a revelation that you will feel and instinctually know is right. If you truly believe in the opportunity, it will be easy to convince others in your organization, as they will be more motivated by your passion than your urgings.

I'm not really sure how this whole revolution thing became so popular in business. I get the winning metaphor, as everyone loves to win and we all adore a winner, but the last time I looked, revolutions were a bloody business. They may ultimately accomplish the intended outcome, but they can really be messy affairs in the process. Every company is different, but at ours, we don't do the revolution thing.

By contrast, revelations are incredibly potent and comparatively clean. It's an incredible feeling to be inspired by something that is surprisingly obvious. You find yourself pausing in the moment so as to fully comprehend what you just learned and suddenly you're compelled to act, not because someone told you what to do, but because your instincts urged you to respond and began to subconsciously move you in the direction of change. As I have shared the wisdom of marketing to age, this is what I have witnessed. The light bulb goes off and people start playing back what I just revealed, which is all part of the process of internalization.

In the end, if you're contemplating marketing to age, don't overthink it and don't overact. You're not here to change the world, and even if you tried, you're probably not going to find enough co-workers to go on the journey with you.

Instead, revel in the revelation and let the wisdom of the idea energize you. You'll be amazed with the power of your passion to transform those around you.

WIN AT THE EDGES

For every marketer who believes that you win by focusing on what's core, there are just as many who believe that one wins by focusing on the edges. The reason for this difference of opinion is that we all have different vantage points. If you're a marketer who has traditionally focused on the core 18- to 49-year-old consumer, a 49+ effort is an edge play. If you already market to the core 49+ consumer, your edge is all about the desire-need states that exist on the periphery of the consumer experience.

The fundamental philosophy behind winning at the edges is two-fold: doing business where no one else is or doing business at the edges of your core to leverage the strength of your core.

While doing business where no one else is typically has a high entry cost, because it's uncontested market space, this approach is sure to lead to fast growth and higher long-term margins. Focusing on the edge of your core is a classic growth strategy as it allows you to leverage the strength of your core in contiguous market spaces. This is sometimes referred to as "expanding the core", but the incremental win takes place on the edge of the core.

Looking at some of today's better-developed brands reveals the significant potential that's inherent in these approaches.

Any idea what the bestselling vehicle is in America? Chances are you would not have guessed Ford's F Series pickup trucks. Yes, it's true. The wildly popular F150 has been the bestselling vehicle in America for the last 32 years, and the bestselling pickup truck for the past 43 years.[52]

This dramatic leadership began when Ford made the first factory-assembled pickup truck in America in 1925. It was based on the Ford Model T design, with a modified rear body. In that Ford chose to make the first pickup truck after years of making the Model T automobile, this was a choice to do business at the edge of the vehicle space where no one else was doing business.

After Ford firmly established its leadership in trucks, it then pushed out from its core (trucks) to do business at the edge of trucks. If you look at the Ford truck line-up today, you can quickly see how and why it has become America's bestselling vehicle. From its humble origins as the "Ford Model T Runabout with Pickup Body", Ford now markets seven different lines of trucks within the F series, beginning with the F150 through the F750 line. Within the F series, they have pushed out to the edges to make trucks for every imaginable light, heavy or super-duty use. Within each of the product lines (eg. F150), they have pushed out to the edges to create different model offerings (eg. The King Ranch model of the F150). If you're in the market for a Ford F-Series truck, you have 29 model choices. If you simply want a F150, you will have five models to choose from, not to mention the myriad cab, box, and engine options within each model. Understanding how to win at the edges has clearly given Ford an edge for years, and more to come.

So what do the edges look like if you decide to market to age? If you're still focused on an 18- to 49-year-old consumer, 49+ is the most massive "edge" that you will ever have the opportunity to market to. For all of the reasons already enumerated in this book, this cohort is both massive and under-leveraged. You will be doing business in an area that's demographically contiguous to your core with a reasonably good chance that you will be doing business where no one else is. You will simultaneously benefit from proximity (an offering that flows from your core) and separation (doing business where others are not).

If you were a marketer of toothpaste to the 18- to 49-year-old cohort, an example of this might be a new paste for those 49+ that offers to rejuvenate teeth and gums to keep them bright and fresh. Still the same core benefit (bright and fresh) with the additional promise of rejuvenation to appeal to the aging consumers on the edge of your core that are being underserved by your prioritization of younger consumers.

If you are already a marketer of toothpaste to the 49+ group that offers to rejuvenate teeth and gums, your edge play would be to offer form variants (gels and rinses) that appeal to the consumers on the periphery of the rejuvenation space who have a strong form preference.

Of course, the goal in all these models is to expand your brand's footprint, but it's critical that you achieve proliferation without complexity. As the market leader, Ford has obviously achieved this balance, but one does need to ask if there's really a need to have an F150 XL and an XLT. Sometimes a simple pruning of the tree will end up producing more fruit.

I'm very fond of the saying, "If you're not living on the edge, you're taking up too much room." It's a not-so-subtle prod to continually innovate for fear of perishing. It's also a reminder that the edge is where you're almost always going to find the next big opportunity. Leading edge? Cutting edge? In the end, it doesn't matter what you call it as long as you are pushing your brand into lucrative contiguous spaces – like aging.

ONLY THE NAMES HAVE BEEN CHANGED

Regardless of your generation, there's a good chance that the name Sergeant Joe Friday rings a bell, as he was a character in one of the most influential television dramas in media history; five decades later, aspects of this series are still familiar, even to those who never took in a single episode. Friday was a beat officer in the popular police drama series *Dragnet* that ran initially in the 1950s and then as a revival from 1967-1970.[53] While memories of the plot lines have long vanished for most, few of us Boomers will forget enduring elements like the ominous four-note introduction to the brass-and-tympani theme song, or still yet, the show's opening narration: "Ladies and gentlemen, the story you are about to see is true. Only the names have been changed to protect the innocent."[54]

A lot of names have changed since the Boomers grew up in a period of unprecedented change. Who doesn't chuckle at the terms our parents used – they certainly seemed normal at the time as we knew no better – but as we reflect they seem downright antiquated. My dad never made the transition from icebox to refrigerator or from Victrola to record player. We grew up with hi-fis, massive pieces of furniture that encased a radio and a Victrola and offered "high fidelity" sound in your choice of maple or walnut. Inevitably, hi-fis gave way to component stereos (I think we "burned the 'furniture'" during the 1970s recession), which then morphed into the home audio systems that we have today. While the names have changed in all of these examples, the core offering and the benefit derived from them has remained constant. Whether it's an RCA Victrola with sound so clear that a dog can hear "his master's voice" or a Sonos smart system of wireless speakers and audio components, one buys them for the pleasure of hearing their favorite sounds. Only the names have changed.

As you go about marketing in the Age of Aging, you're also doing business in a time of high velocity change, obviously driven by extraordinary advances in technology. In that these advances come with new terminology and a process that requires a new language, it's very easy to get seduced into thinking that everything has changed. When that happens, it suddenly feels as though the rug of familiarity has been pulled out from beneath you, that the world of marketing as you once knew it has been turned on its head. You wonder how you could have lost your way in the darkness when everything used to be so clear. Not to worry, you're not alone; we've all been there before.

The way out of the darkness of the smothering cloud of new is to remind yourself that only the names have changed. Streaming providers are simply digitally delivered radio stations and Video on demand (VoD) is just television programming without the *TV Guide*. While everyone loves to say that television is dead, the only thing that's dying is the name "television". Television has been the popular term for an appliance that has been the mainstay mechanism for delivering sight, sound, and motion-based messaging for decades. However, despite the fact that the term television is fading to black and white, our desire for, and enjoyment of, sight, sound, and motion messaging has never been more rampant than it is today, thanks to the proliferation of screens in devices we could not have imagined when we were children watching reruns of *Dragnet* on wood-encased Sylvania's, eating our TV dinners.

What about advances in media? Social media is really nothing more than technologically enhanced word of mouth. Word of mouth is the oldest, most efficient, and most effective medium in the history of marketing. Its formula is simple – it consists only of advocacy and amplification. Someone who likes something is compelled to tell other people about it, and if the recipients of your good word trust you, your message serves as an endorsement of the item, making you an advocate. When you tell more people, or the people you've told tell others, the amplification effect takes hold and before you know it, everyone is clamoring to try the newest object of affection. Social media is simply the digital manifestation of word of mouth – if you "like" something, you are still advocating, as you always have except for the fact that the digital community now does the amplifying. Only the names have changed.

The point of all this is to remind you that the aging consumers are the "innocent" ones; that is, they are a bit naïve when it comes to all the bewildering new names in their world. This is not to say that they are helplessly mired in a time warp of familiar terminology, but rather to say that it is our job as marketers to help them make sense of their modern context. For sure, many of the Boomers are seeking out the latest in technology as a way of self-validating their currency, but just as many are struggling to make sense of the new order. They are either going to embrace it with your help or dismiss it as frivolous if they don't understand it.

Lastly, don't assume that the Boomers are doing things the same way as younger generations simply because they are doing the same things. Take Facebook as an example. On average, Boomers actually spend more time on social media each week than Millennials, but how they spend it differs drastically by generation. The Millennials are always on, engaging superficially throughout the day to stay connected. By contrast, the Boomers are appointment users of social media. They tend to have set times during the day that they go online and stay online to have extended conversations with good friends. This is a case of the name being the same, but the underlying behavior being very different.

Detective Sergeant Joe Friday has also been immortalized for the no-nonsense catch phrase, "Just the facts ma'am." How appropriate. The more bewildering today's complex world gets for the aging consumer, the more they're going to want to simply get to the heart of things, either by retreating to what they know best or by seeking to discover and understand the new. If you're marketing to them today, it would seem as though Detective Friday had the right insight all those many years ago: the names may have changed but they still just want the facts.

GRANT THEM
PERMISSION

The advertising business is notorious for turnover as it's inhabited by restless creative people. Their creative minds are constantly seeking inspiration and when the status quo fails to nourish their need for stimulation, they move on in search of fresh environs to spark their rich imaginations. They arrive at their new destination with a penchant to improve on the creativity of their predecessors (who also left because the status quo underwhelmed them) which they do by imposing new standards and processes that their egos have convinced them is more conducive to the brilliant thinking that they're capable of.

While this is all well and good for the egos of the creative-types, it can wreak havoc on the orderly process that a good agency needs to have to consistently deliver great ideas for its sophisticated clients. Ground zero for this creative tinkering is the creative brief, the document that provides the strategic direction for the development of a communications campaign. If you've ever worked at an agency, chances are you've witnessed the maneuverings of a new creative or strategic planning director as they look to dispense with the old foolish way of doing things to make room for their new mind-blowing approach to world-changing creativity.

Alas, the more creative briefs have changed over the years, the more they've stayed the same. Despite all of the new "look at my way" terminology and formatting, at their core, the elements of the Brief that still do the most to drive strategically sound business building messaging remain essentially unchanged i.e. the benefit, the reason-to-believe and the brand personality. The benefit is an expression of what the brand does for the consumer, the reason-to-believe is something that is true about the product that provides compelling support for why the benefit is true, and the personality is the human qualities ascribed to the brand that make it likeable.

As we seek to get better with marketing to age, we're not going to tinker with this timeless core of the creative brief, with one exception. We're going to advocate the use of permission-to-believe in lieu of reason-to-believe. It may seem like a small dial turn but it's a one-word difference that we believe leads to words that make for much more effective communication.

Let's illustrate the difference by using a category that everyone knows and loves: pizza. If we were marketing Nino's Pizza with the benefit of authentic Italian taste, an example of a reason-to-believe would be that Nino's uses only real ingredients and makes its pizzas the traditional way. In this example, the reason-to-believe is based on reason i.e. some facts that are true that explain that Nino's has an authentic Italian taste because it uses real Italian ingredients and a traditional Italian process.

As we've discussed elsewhere in the book, it's been proven that reason leads to conclusions while emotion leads to action. If this is true, we should be seeking words that lend credence to Nino's authentic taste in a way that engenders some type of emotive (versus logical) response. Something like "Nino's has authentic Italian taste because only Nino's is made with Neapolitan coal-fired ovens that haven't cooled since we were founded in 1972."

In this example, we have offered the consumer some language that is intriguing and suggestive, and since they want to believe that Nino's could be a better pizza, these words give them "permission" to accept their logical tendency. Mind you, there is nothing logical about the relationship between the taste of the pizza and ovens that burn coal and stay hot, but there is just enough going on here to create sufficient interest so as to tip the scales in Nino's favor.

The concept of creating *permission* to believe is particularly important in marketing to age because the aging mind is more prone to remember stories and prose that engenders feeling rather than a litany of facts. Creating permission to believe, because it is less factually anchored to what is true about the product, also gives the creative agency more latitude to create new and different language for an advertising weary Boomer who has heard the ingredient message ad nauseum from an array of too many advertisers for too long. In the end, if your goal is to make the aging consumer a true believer of the wonderfulness of your brand, you can either tell them it's great, or you can let them come to that conclusion on their own. Since most people prefer to buy than to be sold, give them permission to make the choice on their own and you'll end up making a lot of (pizza?) dough.

THERE'S JOY
IN AGING (REALLY)

"How pleasant is the day when we give up striving to be young."
William James, American philosopher.

Yes, you read the headline correctly. Believe it or not, there's scientific proof that there's joy in aging; in fact, it can actually be one of the happiest periods of most people's lives. How can that be? Isn't it depressing to grow old, to lose vitality, to feel the precious remaining years of your life slipping through your fingers?

It's time to forget everything you thought you knew about being a grown-up. Guess what: a 70-year-old has a lot more to be happier about than the typical 30-year-old. According to a recent analysis published by *The Economist*, self-reported wellbeing actually begins to decline after age 18, and reaches a nadir at age 46.[55] People are least happy in their 40s and 50s, but after passing through the nadir, aka the "U-Bend of Life", their outlook steadily improves for the rest of their lives.[56] The things we think make us happy obviously don't.

While different factors affect people differently throughout their lives, there are some common theories as to why happiness improves with age. Most older people are brimming with the confidence and satisfaction of a life well lived. They tend to have a higher level of education and have accumulated a lifetime of wisdom. By now, they know who they are and they know what matters most in life.

Laura Carstensen, a professor of psychology at Stanford University, suggests that this is the result of, "The uniquely human ability to recognize our own mortality and monitor our own time horizons." Because the outlook for the future is not positive, they prefer to live for the present. "They come to focus on things that matter now – such as feelings – and less on long-term goals."[57]

While aging folks can look in the rear-view mirror and reflect on a life well lived, younger adults are facing miles of untraveled road. There is no map for the life that lies ahead. They're mired in the midst of the striving stage of life with omnipresent pressure to keep moving forward and moving up. The essential experience, wisdom, and confidence that they need to succeed are not the province of youth – stress is, and stress is not a recipe for happiness.

We all covet youth because it's a stage of life we've lived and therefore it's one we understand. By contrast, we can't possibly understand aging because most of us aren't there yet. Since we tend to fear things we don't understand, we dread the thought of aging.

If we are to be effective in marketing to age, we will need to suspend our personal beliefs and biases about aging. When it comes to understanding an age stage that we have not yet lived, most of us are guilty of generalizing. Not only are generalizations vague by nature, in this case the prevailing thought that aging is unpleasant is blind thinking.

It's time to look at aging differently, and we can start by running our negative preconceptions through a rose-colored lens of positivity. This book has already elucidated on the optimism that this generation brings to life, and further, we've learned that the aging consumer doesn't want to hear about the problems that your product will fix. The problem with the problem is the problem itself.

Instead, seek to truly understand the positive implications of your product, the benefits it offers to an aging consumer who's already happy and wants to stay that way. Aging consumers are focused on the future of living and longevity, and they are very content in the moment. Look into the future with them and discipline yourself to look for the elusive silver lining, the glass-half-full take on the situation.

If you always look on the bright side of life, you'll see things in a whole new light. You'll see the joy you never knew existed, and you'll become a true believer in the power of positivity.

CREATE DEPTH
WITH LAYERS

A s marketers, we're fond of saying that we're in search of big ideas that are deep in meaning. While a big idea is always better than a small one, and depth is naturally better than being shallow, what we're really saying is that the more deeply our message can resonate with consumers, the more profound its impact will be. If we can find a way deep into their hearts, we will touch their souls and become an eternal part of their lives (or so we believe).

To touch a consumer in a deep way, we must penetrate all the layers that are the essence of their being. We have to appeal to their intellect with a message that has some acceptable level of rationality while also connecting with them viscerally, on some gut level that appeals to them instinctually. To reach them at their hearts, we need to understand their emotional need state and offer them something that appeals to their intuitive feelings. If this all sounds pretty deep (this is just marketing after all) it's because it is; creating ideas that engender deep meaning is a pretty serious endeavor.

While we don't often connect the two, life is really about layers. We come into the world undeveloped and lacking of experience, but as we mature we grow not just by adding years but also by adding layers of life experiences that define who we are. This is true of the total being, but especially of our intellect, which improves by the day as we learn more things. If you think about it, our educational curriculum is a series of layers dosed out to us when we have the aptitude to understand them and then elevated in the next year to keep us learning and growing, grade by grade, layer by layer. Our personal relationships, families, and professional careers all progress in layers, and as our lives advance, we forge identities that are a reflection of the sum-total of the layers. In this regard, a life well lived is one where the layers are truly interrelated and provide the integrity that gives life true meaning.

In Part Two's discussion of how leather gets better with age, we talked about leather's patina being the equivalent of an aging consumer's accumulation of life experiences. Herein, we're illustrating how those same experiences are essentially layered one on top of another, brick by brick as we age. The point of all of this is to say that if you're marketing to age and you want your messaging to connect with the consumer on some deep level, you will need to understand *layers*, not depth.

All too often, marketers try to get deep meaning by looking for "penetrating" insights. In doing so, they're intent on illuminating and understanding what's going on deep inside the consumer's heart and mind, and all too often, they're searching in a place that doesn't give up its secrets easily. Instead of attempting to dive deep for consumer understanding, one must instead proceed layer by layer, one step at a time.

If you're seeking deep understanding, imagine that you're trying to get to the middle of an onion. You would start by peeling off the outermost layer, which would give you a superficial understanding, and as you proceed with each subsequent layer, you would develop not just an understanding of the new layer but also an understanding influenced by that layer's interrelationship with its adjacent layers. You may discover that you've gotten to the heart of the matter after only three layers, hence mission accomplished.

For instance, if you were marketing wearable technology that had the ability to measure one's heart rate, the first layer of understanding would suggest that people are looking for more information about their personal health. The second layer might reveal that they aren't really interested in heartbeat data, but that the investment in the technology helps them feel that they are proactively doing something to be smart about their health. If you keep peeling, you might ultimately reveal that the real reason most people wear these gadgets is to signal to others that they are leading an admirable health-driven lifestyle.

The beauty of the onion approach is that it's methodical and provides new insight with each layer of human understanding that is revealed. By comparison, the penetrating insight approach assumes that the truth you're looking for lies in the deepest reachable layer, and in one's overzealousness to get to the heart of the matter it's often possible to overshoot the most relevant insight.

Since this has been a pretty deep conversation, let's end it on a lighter note. One appetizing way to think of all of this is the notion that, "Life is a piece of cake." After all, a life well lived is really quite delicious because it's made up of so many wonderful layers of goodness. Most aging consumers believe that they have lived a productive life and they're taking the time to reflect, to savor the sweetness of their success.

If you're a marketer who's job it is to understand the lives of the aging consumer – these many metaphorical pieces of layer cake – then you'll want to approach the endeavor one bite at a time. The deep understanding that you're looking for could be right under your nose.

CREATE TIMELESS IDEAS FOR AGELESS PEOPLE

dvertising agencies and their clients are in the same business, but they've always sought different results. The agency is the province of creativity, and it's hard wired to create outlandishly bold, new-to-the-world ideas that will win awards, burnish reputations, and create envy. Intrinsically, they're all about doing something that's never been done before.

Then there are the clients who got an MBA at Wharton instead of an MFA at Parson's School of Design. Ideas are not their be-all and end-all; they're simply a means to an end of meeting established business goals. They're not looking for the big idea that's never been done before as much as they're looking for a proven idea that generates big results. Their holy grail is an established campaign that can run year after year, generating consistently predictable results, and building brand equity at a minimal spending level and agency fee.

While the agency and the client always pretend to be on the same page, they often aren't. It comes down to a simple philosophical difference. The agency says, "We did that before, let's do something else," and the client says, "It worked before, it will work again."

If you're going to get better with age, you and your agency better be on the same page. There's a different way to think about the definition of great advertising that everyone can agree on, especially if you're going to be communicating to Boomers.

Great advertising is about creating timeless ideas that are executed in timely ways.

The notion of timeless ideas reflects several beliefs about advertising. First, that there is a core body of ideas – conceptual approaches and constructs – that are consistently potent and versatile, which means that they work time and time again. They're timeless. Further, a timeless idea doesn't just live in the moment, it is so universally relevant that it has the power to transcend time and run forever.

Despite the proliferation of electronic and digital media that has transpired over the last 50 years, the very first marketing medium is still the most effective one, and the cheapest. It's word of mouth and obviously it's timeless.

What happens when you turn word of mouth into sight, sound, and motion-based messaging to run as a television ad? You get "testimonials", otherwise known as "real people" or "man on the street" advertising. It's arguably the most enduring and timeless of all campaign constructs. I began my career by creating the hidden camera "Restaurant" campaign for Folger's Crystals and I've done one just about every year of my career, and most of them have worked. A lot has changed in our business over three decades, but a lot has stayed the same – timeless ideas are still timeless.

Executing timeless ideas in a *timely* way has never been more vital. Timeliness is about connecting your idea with the consumer at the moment when they are most likely to buy, and it's also about using contemporary connection tactics to improve effectiveness. The two go hand in hand, as contemporary connection techniques are so addressable that it has become super efficient and effective to deliver highly targeted messages to discrete audiences in real time.

Proactiv has become a billion dollar acne-cleaning miracle by embracing the timeless-timely axiom. It has successfully used a people-driven testimonial approach (timeless) that lives online as video content (timely).

If all of this makes sense, imagine what happens when you offer up timeless ideas to a generation that believes they're ageless?

The reality is that most aging consumers don't "get" many of the cutting edge, "timely" ideas that are offered on big-stage programs like the Super Bowl. Most require an understanding of contemporary pop-culture, or use terminology, humor, or film techniques that are beyond their realm of comprehension.

Instead, think within the big box of timeless ideas. How about a powerful human story? Boomers love stories, and the aging mind is better at processing narrative. Music? Music engenders emotion that makes you feel something which for a Boomer is much better than being told something. Jingles? Nostalgia? Bring it.

Don't overcomplicate creativity for the aging consumer. If they see themselves as ageless, they're going to respond to something that's timeless. If you want their money, give them what they want.

DIFFERENTIATE BETWEEN LIFE AND LIVING

W e often use the terms life and living interchangeably, but if you're applying them to the aging consumer, you will need to be sensitive to nuance, as they can have vastly differing interpretations.

One of the consistent themes of this book is the importance of nuance. When it comes to marketing to aging consumers, the devil is in the details. Slight subtleties in the way in which you portray their lives and talk their language can make a big difference in whether your brand is embraced, ignored, or even rejected. The reason is simple: this is a generation that has always preferred the real thing – they expect authenticity and will dismiss you if your message does not ring true.

So what's the difference between life and living? First a familiar caveat: aging is about psychology, and the psychology is irrational. As they see it, life is negative, living is positive. Total nuance. If the Boomers are all about positivity, you need to be too.

Say more? The Boomers see life as the future of living. In this context, life is about their current reality and living is about their optimistic view of what's still possible.

If you put yourself in their shoes to be able to see the world the way they see it, a lot of the reality of their current stage in life has the potential to be unpleasant. Let's face it – the rational aspects of their reality are way too real. Illness, isolation, death? A little too much reality. No thank you.

Instead, human nature takes over and conjures up a scenario that's more pleasant. This is the dynamic that spawns hope and dreams.

Consider that aging consumers have spent most of their existence confronting the ever-present reality of life – the unrelenting challenges of earning a living, raising a family, paying the bills – do not pass Go, do not collect $200. When you're in it up to your ears every day of your adult life, who doesn't dream about those years ahead when you'll be able to break free from endless responsibility and actually live (I'm doing it again right now)? Let's face it, we all do, and the frequency with which we do it increases as we get closer to the time when we actually think we will. If you're a Boomer, most of us think that time is close at hand.

So imagine if your time has finally come, but along with it has come the temptation to worry about your health and longevity. Not petty concerns, but major things that could compromise or shuttle the dreams of your life. Not a chance. The irrational part of your brain takes over and replaces the realities of *life* with the positive scenario – the future of *living*. This explains why the majority of Boomers believe that their best years are still ahead of them.

As they continue to age into this stage of their lives, the Boomers are slowly beginning to accept that the quantity of life remaining is decreasing, so they're compensating by increasing their focus on the quality of life remaining. Quality of life is descriptive of the richness that they intend to bring to *living*.

If you're marketing to aging consumers, the implications are clear. While it's important to be authentic, steer wide of the reality of their lives. Even if your product is made for their age or addresses issues associated with their age, it's best not to be explicit about it. The best course is to ground your message in their needs while skewing the emphasis of your message to the "quality of living" that's possible.

The future of living is inherently about possibilities, and the most optimistic generation that's ever lived is determined to live forever. Impossible? Don't tell them.

CONSULT YOUR DOCTOR IF YOU THINK YOU MAY HAVE BOOMERITIS

Have you ever heard of Boomeritis? If you listened to most of the ads that run on the evening news, you would think that it was a common ailment afflicting all aging people with symptoms including arthritis, erectile dysfunction, irritable bowel syndrome, incontinence, high blood pressure, hot flashes, dryness and itching, and God forbid, a loss of sexual drive. Think again.

Boomeritis is a term widely used by the medical community to describe the physical consequences of engaging in activities that are inappropriate for your age. When are most cases of Boomeritis diagnosed and treated? Monday morning. You see where this is going – the generation that coined the phrase "weekend warriors" is fighting aging every step of the way, with one footnote: the steps are usually measured in kilometers.

They are taking to the streets, the gyms, the yoga studios, and their bikes by the millions, hell-bent with fury to defy aging by defining their bodies. There's a large cohort of Boomers – the "Me, My Body" segment – whose orientation to life is physical and who believe that a healthy body is the key to a productive life. They worship physical activity with a "body as temple" spirit and they have convinced themselves that there is a direct correlation between physical fitness and longevity.

My first boss in advertising – back in the *"Mad Men"* days – was a portly gentleman who earned the moniker "The Lord of Lunch" for his legendary midday dining escapades (when did any work get done back in those days?). The Lord was quite proud of his culinary lifestyle and physique and was once heard to say, "I don't play any sports that require special shoes." Flash-forward and it amazes me to think that most Boomers not only own a special pair of shoes, they probably own a special pair for each of their different physical activities.

I have a lot of fun with this topic when I travel the speaking circuit. I'll often ask an audience of Boomers a multiple-choice question like the following:

If you bike 30 miles on a Saturday and your legs ache at the end of the day, you should:

a) Consider a different type of exercise.
b) Bike fewer miles next time.
c) Curse yourself for not being in shape and bike 40 miles on Sunday.

You guessed it – the audience always chooses C and adds a gratuitous "duh" as if to suggest that the answer was obvious (idiot).

What's going on here? The symptoms of Boomeritis are physical, but the cause is psychological. The obsession with fitness is driven by a combination of rational and irrational beliefs.

Rationally, many aging people have discovered that physical activities are both enjoyable and beneficial. Taking advantage of their increased discretionary time, their morning commute is a drive to a pilates class where they can enjoy a physical workout and social time with classmates. Many of these physically oriented folks are also pleasure seekers who love to exercise because it makes them feel great all day long, while also taking away the guilt of having that extra glass of pinot noir with dinner. Physicality is an essential ingredient for their "quality of living".

Irrationally, many of these people believe that the more they push themselves, the better they will feel and the longer they will live. Obviously, there's a medical correlation between physical health and longevity, but Boomeritis has different root causes. The determination to be so exercise-and-activity driven moves in correlation with one's sense of diminishing longevity. Said another way, the shorter life seems, the longer the workout. Behold the irrational reality of Boomeritis.

What do you do with this? File Boomeritis under "irrational insights". If this is how they see themselves in the context of how they view life, then this is the imagery that you need to reflect in your brand. The clichéd images of retirees gardening in the backyard need to be replaced with Boomers wearing special shoes during the bike stage of the triathlon. This is an iconoclastic generation if there ever was – their spirit will always remain "never say die", even if they kill themselves in the process.

DON'T CUT THE TAIL OFF THE DOG

My former boss at Saatchi & Saatchi, chairman Bob Seelert, had a quick wit and a great way with words. He always seemed to have an apt adage to put things in a different perspective, and it was usually just what was needed to bring clarity and consensus to the room. While most people are content to parrot timeworn clichés, Bob always seemed to have fresh material. Leave it to Bob to create a bespoke version of the proverbial "dog chasing his tail" expression.

In his first book – *Start with the End in Mind* – Bob cautions against "cutting the tail off the dog one inch at a time". This is something that those of us in the advertising business had experienced over and over again, but had failed to understand absent these vivid words. Cutting the tail off the dog one inch at a time is what happens when a series of seemingly small and insignificant changes have a cumulative effect that is catastrophic.

Let's pretend that the new product department at the company High as a Kite has just unveiled a new, lightweight kite made of a special polymer that allows it to reach flying heights not previously attainable with conventional kites. The executive team is impressed and they approve funding to "launch" the kite in time for next year's kite-flying season. From here, the new kite project will be managed by a matrix of teams so that all the expertise needed for a successful launch can be applied.

As each department "adds value" to the new kite, they make incremental "improvements" to the concept. Research and development (R&D) decides to use a heavier polymer to prevent tearing, Procurement sources cheaper strut material to reduce cost of goods. Sales makes a few small design changes to respond to customer demands, and marketing adds a miniature camera to capture high altitude content to use on YouTube. You see where this is going. The kite gets launched, only it won't fly because it's too heavy. The final design bears no resemblance to the original concept.

High as a Kite now has a disaster on its hands, and the executive team wants answers. Not surprisingly, everyone denies responsibility and the finger pointing begins. In the end, no one department is responsible for the catastrophic consequence because each department believes that its small change was not significant enough to have contributed to the enormity of the product failure. Each admits to having only cut an inch of the dog's tail, and none of them believe they are responsible for the ugly dog that is now missing his entire tail.

This is an amusing little story, but surely all of you have experienced this very scenario at least once if not several times during your career, and it was likely not a laughing matter. How can something so simple and obvious get repeated so often by so many businesses?

Part of the answer can be found in the title of Bob's book: they fail to keep the end in mind. The rest of the answer has to do with human nature and corporate culture.

For almost all of us, jobs are life support. We work and are motivated to succeed by the need to earn an income that will provide the food and shelter that sustains life. With so much at stake, it's human nature to want to prove one's worth in the organization by adding personal value to projects. Too many people adding small doses of value adds up to too much value-added.

It's the responsibility of the corporate culture to guard against this phenomenon, but if the company's structure, decision-making hierarchy or accountability is flawed in any way, there's a good chance that you're going to end up with a lot of ugly pooches.

If you're going to market to age, you're going to need one incredible dog. The Boomers are marketing's most deeply experienced and knowledgeable consumers, so they know the real thing when they see it, and vice versa.

Because marketing to age may well be without precedent for you and the rest of the humans in your corporate culture, you'll need to make sure that everyone keeps the end in mind throughout the entire process. The best way to keep everyone focused on the same end is to make sure everyone has the same map. A vision is not the same thing as a map, because a vision is subjective and is open to interpretation. A map says "X marks the spot", and when you get there, your loyal dog Spot will be right by your side, tail and all.

WISDOM GETS
BETTER WITH AGE

W e've all heard the expression "older and wiser too". While it's an expression that's been around for years and is perilously trite, if you're an aging consumer it's a phrase that only gets better with age. No one talks about wisdom when they're young – it just doesn't seem to be the right word to describe our mental aptitude when we have snappier options like brains, smarts, and intelligence. For sure, wisdom is an asset that's reserved for older folks and we're only too happy to keep it all to ourselves.

Anyone who is wise is intelligent, but not all intelligent people are wise. Ponder that. In the beginning, all of us are born with the gift of intellect and throughout our lives, we have honed that asset through human experience and education until one day we are deemed to be intelligent. Intelligent people tend to excel at life's endeavors because they are able to leverage their superior mental aptitude and powers of reason. Smart people tend to do well, and this dynamic usually continues through middle age and beyond.

What distinguishes wisdom from intelligence is experience – wisdom equals intelligence plus experience. While there are a lot of highly intelligent young people in all walks of life, because they are young – and through no fault of their own – they fundamentally lack the life experience that only comes with years. It's one thing to learn something, but it's another thing to learn through experience. As a child, we're told not to touch the hot stove, but until we experience what it feels like to be burned, we haven't really learned the lesson. The intelligence or reasoning part of our young brains tells us that heat is dangerous, but our experience with heat creates wisdom that reminds us that heat is painful.

We have described aging in many different ways throughout this book, but the common thread that explains why we get better with age is the value of accumulated experiences. We're "older and wiser too" because the percentage of our total intelligence that has been shaped by experience increases as we age. This is why people of age are often heard saying things like, "There's nothing I haven't seen before" or "Been there, done that." This is their way of saying, "I know that because I have lived that." This is an advantage of perspective and context that younger people simply will not develop until they age further.

In marketing to age, it's important that you know that aging folks are wise and that because they're wise, they know they're wise. As such, it's imperative that your brand reflects an understanding of them that respects this prowess. Their wisdom is a source of pride because most of them have earned it over the course of a lifetime that's been filled with challenges, perseverance, and success. It is a gift of age – no different than the beauty of youth – that they secretly hope gets noticed and perhaps even praised. So be equally as wise and do whatever you can to recognize and appreciate that age has its advantages. While this is not to suggest that you "respect your elders" (don't forget that it was the elders who told us to respect elders), it is suggesting that you respect their wisdom if for no better reason than it's the intelligent thing to do.

MAKE HAY WHILE THE SUN SHINES

I'm guessing that this is a bit of a quaint phrase that's meaning may not be immediately evident to most readers. If I explained that it was one of my dad's more favorite expressions, you're probably still no closer to deciphering its meaning either. The truth be told, I learned what these words meant the hard way, by growing up on a farm where we literally made hay while the sun shined. So by now you're surely asking what on earth does working the land have to do with marketing to aging consumers?

The phrase "make hay while the sun shines" is an expression of opportunistic intent. It is about a state of preparedness, a readiness to act when conditions are ideal. It implies that if one does the right thing at the right time, then the results will be ideal.

In the world of farming, the making of hay requires a sustained period of sunny weather, beginning with the cutting of the fresh grass that is left to dry in the hot sun. After the top layer has dried sufficiently, the soon-to-be hay is then flipped over to expose the underside to the sun's rays. When the full drying process is complete, the hay is then raked into windrows to be converted into bales. The bales are then removed from the field and transported back to the farm where they are put up into the haymow of the barn. To this day – despite great modernization and mechanization of the technique – the making of hay is still often referred to as "putting *up* the hay".

The aforementioned process – assuming the average farmer is not busy milking his herd twice a day and doing everything else required to maintain a farming operation – takes about five days. While the presence of sunshine is initially required to dry the freshly cut green grass, the subsequent haying process requires its continued presence to ensure that the hay does not get exposed to any moisture. Wet hay presents two unacceptable risks to the farmer: it can rot in the mow, or worse yet, it can trigger spontaneous combustion that has been the cause of many catastrophic barn fires.

So at least as it relates to making hay, you're hopefully starting to understand the meaning of the expression. The making of hay is highly opportunistic. If the farmer believes that he will have a stretch of favorable weather, all resources are committed to action for an urgent and timely response. On a farm, this is the naval equivalent of "all hands on deck". If you're the hands, there's nothing pleasant about this type of hot, dusty, nonstop work.

If you look at the big picture of marketing to age – particularly with the Boomers who have recently exited the 18- to 49-year-old demographic in their entirety – we clearly have an opportunity to "make hay while the sun shines". We have a window to be opportunistic, to take advantage of the underleveraged potential of the aging cohort and to do so to bide time until the Millennials show up in full force on or around 2030. We have a period of time while the Boomers are still earning and spending income and feeling younger than their years. If you embrace the importance of marketing to age, this is prime time, the time is now, and the sun is shining on us. Sure, we have many years ahead of us to "make hay" in marketing to age, but if you're smart, you'll take advantage of today's favorable circumstances to get started. While your competition tries to find the proverbial needle in the haystack aka solving the Millennial riddle, you can be putting up lots of hay. Marketing in today's highly competitive environment can feel like an endless winter, but if you're making hay on the aging market when others aren't, you'll be enjoying the warmth of sunshine all year long.

DON'T MARKET TO THEIR MALADIES

Marketers make lots of things to help people deal with the symptoms associated with aging, and let's face it, we're grateful for all of the modern advances in medicine. If I'm an aging consumer, the more the merrier. Longevity has increased and so has quality of life, so what's not to like?

What's not to like is how most of the marketing of these beneficial products – and for the most part, we mean pharmaceutical or over-the-counter offerings – make the aging consumer feel. Yes, products that were manufactured to make you feel better can actually make you feel bad in the process. How so?

By way of an example, I was recently asked to participate in a gathering of pharmaceutical companies as an expert on the aging consumer. One of the companies was looking for insight to market a new product designed to alleviate the discomfort caused by dryness. As is classically done, they were looking to determine whether dryness or discomfort was the best way in – which of the two problems (or both?) does the consumer want us to solve? My response? Neither.

If you have a product that addresses symptoms that are caused by age, your marketing needs to be extremely sensitive to the emotional context of the symptom. If you're too blunt in marketing to their malady, you will unintentionally remind them that they're getting old, and worse, that you lack empathy for their condition.

So back to our pharmaceutical marketers making a choice between dryness or discomfort. When I first suggested that they focus on neither, they were aghast. How could an alleged "expert" offer such misguided advice? By the time I had explained my rationale, the light bulbs went on over their heads one at a time.

My advice was simple yet poignant. Instead of focusing on the symptoms of aging, you need to focus on the psychology of aging. When you're a marketer, aging is about psychology – not physiology – and the psychology is irrational.

Nodding, they then asked, "So what is the psychology surrounding this age-related dryness and discomfort?" You can only get the answer right if you ask the question the right way. The relevant question is, "What is the psychology of aging that's caused by the dryness and discomfort (that's caused by aging)?" More nods.

The psychology that's at play in this instance is the consumer's desire to feel normal, to be treated normally by others, and to enjoy an uncompromised quality of life. As such, the marketing message needs to begin by reflecting an empathetic understanding of the consumer, accompanied by positivity and joy.

At the end of the day, some minor dryness and discomfort is not a big deal, and because she is determined to not let it define her, she is already prone to rising above the condition so she can go beyond. Your marketing needs to tap into this positive psychological momentum, and move with it. When you focus on the problem that your product is trying to solve, you end up fighting the tide of positive emotion that she has brought to her condition.

Does this mean that you can't talk about what your product does? Of course not. Like most smart marketing, it's a question of balance. The product's attributes and benefits need to be seen as a means to the end of an uncompromised life, which is different than a solution that solves dryness and discomfort.

So how is it that so many really bright marketers unknowingly end up marketing to maladies? For starters, there is an incredible amount of R&D and organizational investment involved in bringing many of these products to market. When you spend years and years dwelling on your product's dryness and discomfort performance attributes, there's a pretty good chance that that's the orientation you're going to bring to marketing. The key here is to create demarcation between the manufacturing and marketing aspects of the initiative. When it comes time to market, you will need a major paradigm shift in favor of solutions, not problems.

One of the other key reasons that brands market to maladies is that they don't know what they don't know – marketing to age needs a big time focus on the small nuances. If you truly want to penetrate the mind-set of aging consumers, you'll need to keep digging until you reach a deep understanding of what really matters to them – the positive psychology of aging.

GET THE NEW NEWS
ON OLD HABITS

There's a lot of perception versus reality that comes into play when marketing to age, and most of it is misperception. The most common myth about aging consumers is also the one that prevents most brands from targeting them – they are old and stuck in their ways. Nothing could be further from the truth.

According to research findings published by Nielsen and BoomAgers, aging consumers are no more or less brand loyal than their younger counterparts. Said another way, they tend to be more similar than dissimilar with one significant exception. The Baby Boomers control 70% of US disposable income and they dominate 119 of 123 consumer-packaged goods (CPG) categories – a staggering 94%. That's big new news on old habits.

So what's driving such a massive misperception? Cultural inertia. We live in a country that covets youth and prefers new to old. Because we see youth as such a desirable state and stage of life, we tend to roll old stereotypes forward and apply them to the current generation of aging people. While there may have been a time when people in their 60s were curmudgeonly, stubborn, and sedentary, it simply isn't true any more. The fact that we've added 30 years to life expectancy in the last 100 years means that today's 65-year-old is a very different person.

Aside from being physically and emotionally different versus the cultural bias of age, older consumers are defying past patterns of behavior because they're bringing a different set of generational values to this stage of their lives. Their generational values – a personal set of beliefs about the way the world should be, formed during their formative years – do more to influence their behavior than physical age.

These core values drive a psychology to aging that compensates for the physical realities of aging. Since society's stereotype of aging is in conflict with their more idealistic view of aging, they adapt by saying and doing things that validate their desired self-image. Therefore, if they worry that others might see them as old and set in their ways, they may deliberately go out of their way to change established patterns of behavior or buy the latest in fashion so they are seen as contemporary and vital.

There are other myths of aging that are simply misperceptions. How about the belief that older people slow down and sit back? Or the belief that an older consumer lacks mental acuity. Honestly?

For the same reason that they subconsciously fight the stereotype of being old and set in their ways, the aging consumer is determined to stay active and mentally fit.

Not only are they not stopping, they're actually just getting started. With Baby Boomers leaving the traditional workplace at the rate of 10,000 a day for the next 15 years, they're starting a brand-new stage in their lives, a stage that will bring the kind of dramatic lifestyle change that they haven't seen since graduating from college or starting a family. These are exciting times that are so ripe with opportunity that most Boomers are gearing up for what's next, not gearing down.

This new stage of life is also a time for reinvention, a creative rethinking of one's station in life. After years of a somewhat predictable existence dictated by the patterns of career and family, the Boomers are now enjoying not only more freedom of time but also a liberation of mind. How many older people do you know who retired early, only to come back a year later, desperate for the constant intellectual stimulation and purpose that comes from work? With so many pre-retirement Boomers indicating that they will continue to work after retirement, the concept of "retirement" is dangerously close to becoming a non-concept. Retirement has become a quaint concept, and as its relevance fades away, the myths of social withdrawal and physical and intellectual degradation that accompanied it will disappear as well.

Here's another instance where the clichés have become reality. Indeed, the Boomers are defying convention and rewriting the rules of aging, just as they re-wrote the rules as they came of age in the '60s. Forget what you thought you knew about aging, because it's old news. The Boomers are still in the headlines still doing new things that are making the news.

AIRPLANE MODE?

I recently found myself on an Air France flight preparing to return home to the States after a week of business in Europe. As the boarding process continued, an older, attractively dressed woman sat down in the seat next to me and began to prepare herself for the long flight ahead. A short time thereafter, the boarding door closed and the flight attendant got on the speaker system and went through the usual pre-flight disclaimers, including the need for everyone to promptly put their phones in airplane mode.

As I reached to disable my phone, I noticed the older woman sitting next to me fidgeting nervously with her iPhone. As she began to get somewhat exasperated, she summoned a nearby flight attendant to her seat. Despite my limited grasp of the French language, it was immediately clear what the passenger was asking: "Qu'est-ce que c'est airplane mode?"

While it only took a moment for the flight attendant to cheerfully walk the passenger through her settings menu, I instead pondered what I had just witnessed for another ten minutes or so. Sure, we all have our moments with technology and feel embarrassed to ask what we think are dumb questions (at least the Genius Bar at the Apple store makes me feel smart), but there was something about this particular scene that puzzled me. Ah, perhaps it was her first day with a new iPhone, or perhaps it was her first flight with an old iPhone, but actually, not really. I'm pretty sure that she simply didn't know how to do very much with her new telephone that was brimming with extraneous smart technology.

Before I continue, let me be very clear. By nature, I am not critical; I simply observe. That's what advertising people do for a living, so we're always "people watching" and looking for insights into human behavior. You see, my flying companion did not acquire her Apple iPhone 6 to take advantage of the myriad technological wonders that it is capable of, she bought it so she could confirm for herself that she was up to date on the latest young things in the world. Technology is a virtual fountain of youth for the aging consumer because hand-held technology conspicuously epitomizes modernity. So I'm thinking that despite needing to ask a flight attendant a silly question about a smartphone, this woman still felt pretty darned good about herself as she looked forward to touching down in New York City where the price of social currency is almost as high as her native Paris.

When I shared this story with a friend of mine, she chuckled and explained that her mother, who lives in Florida, has been dying to get an iPhone (not a new cell phone, her *first* cell phone) despite the fact that she apparently still doesn't know how to operate a microwave. Why the sudden interest to get an iPhone? All of her friends have one and they're getting pictures of the grandchildren faster than she is. For the aging consumer, technology is about currency, not capability.

So the point of this story is that where one boarding door closes, another opens. The technology that we take for granted today is truly one of the contemporary wonders of the world. It's wonderful to think of all the ways that technology can improve our lives, even though for some of us it's just about having it in our lives.

STRATEGY IS ABOUT CHOICE – CHOICE HELPS YOU WIN

A t a time when marketing has become obsessed with modern connection tactics, there's never been a better time for an emphasis on strategy. All the best execution in the world cannot overcome lackluster strategic thinking.

While this book is incapable of helping you to create a highly successful strategy for your unique endeavor, we can at least establish some principles of effective strategy, beginning with some clarity around what strategy is and is not.

While there have been countless volumes written on this topic, none is more insightful than A.G. Lafley and Roger Martin's *Playing to Win: How Strategy Really Works.*

Lafley and Martin observe that while most companies believe they have a strategy, what they actually have is a vision or a plan, which are only elements of a strategy.[60] Instead, they define strategy as being about the specific choices that need to be made to win in the marketplace. They go on to say that, "Strategy therefore requires making explicit choices – to do some things and not others – and building a business around these choices. In short, strategy is choice."[61]

One of the critical strategic choices you will need to make is "where to play". Presumably you're reading this book because you're intrigued by the potential in playing in the uncontested space of marketing to age. As compelling as the case is for marketing to this audience, what tends to get in the way is the difficulty of choice – making a choice to do one thing and not another is hard.

While it's common belief that many businesses misstep because they made a wrong choice, the reality is that many err because they failed to make any choice at all. The Achilles' heel of many corporate cultures is their earnestness, overconfidence, and desire to please. When this is the operative mentality, everyone "signs up" to get it done and nothing gets done well because they've all bitten off more than they can chew. As Lafley and Martin point out, it's hard enough to win these days, yet alone trying to win when you haven't prepared yourself properly.

When it comes to marketing to age, you will need to make some fundamental but critical choices. Let's borrow from Lafley and Martin and frame these up as "where to play" choices. By way of an example, a Cadillac Escalade and a Jeep Cherokee are both SUVs but that's where the similarities end. The Escalade is built for the urban sophisticate while the Cherokee is the SUV of choice for the off-road adventurer. They've each made a very discrete choice about where they are going to play in the automotive space, and both are winning. By contrast, assuming you worked in the automotive business, how many times have you been in a meeting where marketing proclaims a desire to be the best vehicle for off-road adventure but without alienating sophisticated urban buyers? The "but" is the giveaway that a choice is being ignored.

In marketing to age, your choice begins with *who* – who is the specific consumer that I'm targeting and what are the category needs unique to that consumer? Let's use women's hair care as an example. Is she an aging woman with dry, brittle hair? A woman who's coloring grey hair? One who's transitioning from colored hair to natural? One who has grey hair and wants it to look its best? All of these are examples of aging women who have hair-care needs, but the "where to play" is very different depending on *who* she is.

In the world of marketing, the *who*, *what*, and *how* choices are all important, but none is more critical than getting the who choice right. When you can get clarity as to who your consumer is, most of the other choices seem to fall naturally into place. If she's a woman transitioning from coloring to her natural color, I now know I'm going to need a regimen-based offering that will help her with transitional hair care over time, including a product that helps her new, natural look be at its best on day one.

As easy as this sounds, the most fundamental failure in marketing strategy is the failure to make a specific choice on the *who*. This behavior is a consequence of mass marketing mentality, which has marketers seeking to maximize the number of potential consumers for whom their offering will be appealing. If you're marketing to age in well-established product categories, you should be looking to optimize, not maximize. You're never going to, nor should you try to, get 76 million aging Baby Boomers to love what you're selling. The philosophy of optimization is all about making a choice, the choice that will allow you to sell the optimal amount of product for the given consumer opportunity you have chosen. If you do that well, you'll win, and when you win, you will have earned the opportunity to make additional choices to extend your brand with other optimized offerings for other consumers. Behold the power of choice.

ACT YOUR AGE

One of the questions that BoomAgers, my agency, gets asked most often is how to cast talent for advertising targeted to the aging consumer – do you cast people that look like them so they can "see themselves in the mirror" or do you cast younger people because all older people like younger imagery? The answer is both.

When it comes to choosing talent to represent your brand, you need to act your age. Sounds simple in theory, but it can be challenging in practice.

While most brands have a well-defined target audience, it's usually expressed as a range of ages so as to align with media buying audience definitions, such as women aged 25 to 54. When it comes time to cast for that ad, you and your advertising agency will now need to make a choice.

Since it's human nature to choose the path of least resistance, most marketers and their agencies design a work-around for this dilemma: they create and cast for advertising a range of talent so they can depict a range of ages that's aligned with the target audience. But let's say you're running a beauty business and you're in need of a single "face" for your brand. What then? You'll need to make a choice and choice is hard.

If you're marketing to age, here are some tips to make the choice simple. For starters, you need to remember that age is not a number. Ignore the fact that you have a numerically defined target audience and instead focus on the *spirit* of your consumer. Conjure up everything you've read in this book thus far to get at the essence of how your consumer sees themself at this stage of their life, and just as importantly, what they aspire to do as they age. Add a paragraph to your strategy statement that's called "Her Spirit" and be sure that everyone on your team and at your agency has a crystal clear understanding of what she's "all about at her age".

Next up, don't forget that the Boomers are a generation that expects and respects authenticity from the brands they love. They are not looking for *your* beliefs about who they are, how they should behave and what they look like – they are looking to see *their* beliefs and *their* sense of self-identity manifested in your message.

Lastly, not only is aging not numerical, it's also not biological. Instead, aging is psychological and the psychology is irrational. Your casting – and its portrayal of your brand – needs to reflect what you have learned about her unreasonable view of her age and aging. Simply put, she feels younger than she looks, so when she sees an image that matches hers, she thinks young.

When you roll all this up, the best way to think about casting for the aging consumer is with an objective of "aspirational authenticity". While this may seem borderline oxymoronic, it is actually a paradoxically potent set of words.

Aspirational authenticity is grounded in authenticity for all of the reasons already mentioned, but also to protect against a portrayal of the aging consumer that strays a little too close to reality. The aspirational adjective ensures that it is a depiction of authenticity that helps the brand to live in a world that has all of the positivity and joy that the optimistic aging consumer lives every day.

While the intent of these guidelines is to steer you in the right direction, remember that the aging target is a moving target. As you seek to "act their age", remember that they are continually redefining their lives as they look to rationalize the developments that come with age. With so many moving pieces, it's critical that you have an understanding of them that's grounded in what's constant – their enduring personal values. As a generation that is widely regarded to be the most optimistic ever, acting their age by being aspirationally authentic is going to look a lot like what they feel like when they look in the mirror.

BE POPULAR BY UNDERSTANDING THE POP CULTURE OF AGING

W ithout a doubt, the single question that I get asked most often by the aging consumer is, "How come I don't get the ads on tv anymore?" The frequency with which I hear this lament tends to increase around the airing of the Super Bowl. Care to guess what's going on here?

For starters, let's agree that there's some exaggeration at play in this query. The aging consumer obviously still understands most of the advertising that they see on television, but their annoyance with the ones they don't comprehend is having a disproportionate effect. The work they don't get is especially irritating to them because it's serving as confirmation of two other things that are troubling them i.e. they're subconsciously worried that their age might be affecting their mental acuity and currency, or worse, that they're being de-prioritized by marketers in favor of youth.

Most of the ads that they're struggling with are likely to be campaigns created for Prime time, the 8:00pm to 11:00pm viewing slot where pricing and audience delivery place a premium on delivering a younger 8-34 year-old audience with best-in-class creativity. No other prime time event is more widely watched than the Super Bowl, aka "advertising's greatest stage".

When agencies are tasked with creating campaigns that will be aired in television's most expensive dayparts, the premium price of the ad space puts a premium on creativity. Agency creative teams have to dig deep to come up with their best ideas and they usually do so with a bias toward popular culture, celebrities, humor and youth. They get what they get, so their tendency is to lead with what they know and like.

If you've ever told a joke in the presence of a young child who doesn't get the punch line (it's not their fault, it's "above" them) then you can appreciate that the reverse is likely to happen when a 20-something agency creative comes up with a humorous campaign idea for prime time; the joke is now "beneath" the older viewers who may see it. Even if the humor is on the same intellectual par of age, there's a pretty good chance that the style of humor is new, and in that it's something an older viewer has not been in on lately (think slang), chances are they're not going to get it.

When I'm asked to define aging, I'll often quip that aging is what happens when you don't recognize the people in *People* magazine anymore (do people still read magazines?). Obviously, *People* is a popular entertainment manifestation of pop culture, and pop culture is by definition about that which is in the mainstream, or more likely, the emerging mainstream. Let's call it for what it is; the aging consumer is many things, but by and large, they don't live in or influence the cultural mainstream. Advertising that is inspired by images and events that live in this stream are not going to connect with an aging consumer, and if you don't care to connect with them, that's one thing. If you do – and you should – then you'll need a different approach.

Simply put, if you want them to get your product, they'll need to get your advertising. To do that well, you'll need to get something else – you'll need to get in touch with what the aging consumer enjoys in *their* popular culture i.e. the popular culture of aging. To do this, you don't need to redefine popular culture, you simply need to translate it differently. The most common elements that shape pop culture are entertainment, movies, sports, news, politics, fashion, technology and even advertising itself. To reflect the pop culture of aging, you need to understand it, which is easily enough done if you simply spend time with the aging consumer to understand what's current and most popular within the aforementioned categories. This isn't hard to do, but it doesn't happen as often as it should. This is because there's a bias to think of popular culture as being a mainstream phenomenon, and if it's mainstream, it must be young. By this point, this book has hopefully demonstrated that aging is the new mainstream. The size and value of the aging consumer is so meaningful relative to the balance of the population, that to think of it as anything but the main event is a big, big miss. At the end of the day, while marketing and advertising are about increasing sales, they're also about creating popularity. The most transformative campaigns in the business are those that create skyrocketing sales by making something irresistible and pervasive, and they do it by having an ultra keen sense of what it is within the pop culture that influences popularity, right now. When it comes to aging, very few marketers are asking this question today because the notion is still relatively new. So right now is your chance – your opportunity to become the most popular brand in your category by understanding what the popular culture of aging enjoys most. Marketing is a popularity contest, and the aging consumer knows a winner when they see one.

KNOW WHEN
TO STOP

I recently participated in a conference attended by some of the top executives in the world and when they were asked to share their single most important piece of advice for success, almost all of them said the same thing: fail quickly. If it's true that we fail more than we succeed, and that we learn more from our failures than our successes, then a smart leader is one who recognizes that his company is going to fail and prepares accordingly. Failure is in fact inevitable and at some level needs to be regarded as acceptable. But what's not acceptable is to allow pockets of failure to linger and slowly bring about the demise of the entire enterprise.

In a day and age when the speed of technology and innovation can render successful businesses obsolete virtually overnight, some smart companies are choosing to send their executive teams to wilderness survival schools. The wilderness is a place where the predictable patterns of daily life do not operate, and where one mistake often triggers a series of cascading consequences that can prove to be fatal. In this environment, management and even leadership skills are typically insufficient. Instead, one needs to understand the principles of survival – how to successfully compensate for some element of failure in the wilderness to ensure safety; said another way, how to fail quickly and then get back on track.

Instructors at some survival schools use the acronym STOP to train their candidates. It stands for Stop, Think, Observe and Plan.[62] Imagine a backpacker who's on what he thinks is a routine hike until he finds himself off track. He doubles back to where he thinks he made the wrong turn, takes what he thinks is the right path, only to find himself confused once again. He begins to wander around aimlessly and gets even more mired, to the point where he is now officially lost. If he has a fair amount of wilderness experience he has a reasonably good chance of finding his way to safety, but many do not. Their little problem (where am I?) tends to turn into a big problem (it's snowing, I'm hypothermic, I'm going to die), because it's human nature to press onward to get to the intended destination as soon as possible. They fail to survive because they forget to STOP.

As you're on the journey to market to age, you're bound to take a few wrong turns, which is both inevitable and acceptable. However, if you embrace the importance of failing quickly, you will self-arrest any further action that could deepen your dilemma. A smart marketer will take the time to stop, which in today's fast-paced environment is an act that most people avoid. Instead, we press on, blindly convinced that we'll figure things out on the move that most times only moves us farther from our destination.

If you're disciplined enough to stop, it will give you the opportunity to clear your head and think objectively about your predicament. You will take time to observe where you are, see what is around you, and what lies ahead. This will provide you with the vital intelligence that you'll need to have a plan that you can act on to get to safety. People who are lost in the wilderness rarely survive because their meanderings fortuitously led them in the right direction, or because they got lucky. They survive because they prepared to survive by creating a plan.

It sounds so obvious but it's not. So much of success in life and in business is counterintuitive, and in this case, we've learned that survival in perilous conditions is about stopping versus moving forward. If the wilderness metaphor feels a bit extreme, think again. There are entire business categories that are currently lost because of shifting demographics and generational values (think McDonald's in a deep forest of Chipotles). If your only strategy is to press on in the general direction that you were heading in before you got lost, then there's a good chance that your situation will only become increasingly dire. If you aspire to have a long successful future – and most of us do – then time is fundamentally on your side. Most of us have more time than we realize, so if you want to keep moving ahead, there's no better time to STOP.

DON'T LET THE DIGITAL TAIL WAG THE IDEA DOG

I f you're going to communicate to Boomers, you're going to need to use digital marketing tools. In so doing, you'll want to make sure that digital tactics don't drive the core brand idea.

To the amazement of many, the Boomers are surprisingly digital. While they aren't leading the digital revolution, their sheer numbers are the power behind the rapid growth in digital technology. They are all too eager to adopt the newest thing, as all that is cutting edge serves as their virtual fountain of youth. The internet serves up connectivity to a generation that's intent on staying vibrant and mentally and socially vital.

Statistically, their digital engagement continues to grow rapidly, led by their use of social media, which has more than tripled in the last four years, from 13% of all Boomers to 43%.[63] They're spending 27 hours per week on social media, 10% more than the Millennials, and 53% of them are on Facebook.[64] Go figure.

That's at least one good reason to include digital in your aging consumer media mix. You must reach them where they are, and they're on digital in a big way. Another reason is the inherent efficiency and addressability of digital media. The Boomers are a massive mass audience so, practically speaking, you're probably going to want to focus your media buy on a high potential subset reached digitally.

Now, about that idea dog with the digital tail. Most dogs I know wag their tails. I've yet to meet many tails, yet alone tails that wag their dogs. As such, I'm inclined to respect the natural order of things.

In marketing, the natural order of things has been to understand consumer behavior, create big ideas, and then connect those ideas with consumers when and where they're most likely to be receptive to your message. Everyone in marketing speaks a different language, but this is the basic translation that has been the modus operandi in the industry for years.

Along with the advent of digital technology came the proliferation of new language and new processes. If you were a "digital native", you spoke the language and drove the process. If you were a marketer still tied to the analog model, you had no choice but to feign understanding, and ultimately seek comprehension by hiring an "interpreter", aka a digital ad agency.

The rise of digital and the specialist agencies that service it have created real division within the advertising business – a division of philosophy and practice.

The traditionalists believe that the best process starts with identifying insights that explain consumer behavior, creating ideas that reflect the insight and differentiate the brand in a meaningful and enduring way, and expressing the ideas in the media that make the most sense for the idea and can connect with the consumer when and where they're most receptive to the message. All of this is fundamentally an idea-centric approach.

The digitalists – because they were born with digital media – have a bias to start at the media end of the process. They are keen to understand what consumers are doing online and to know what conversations they're a part of. From there, they look to insinuate a brand message into the conversation to take advantage of the inertia inherent in the conversation. It's a connection-centric approach.

Which one's right? It depends on whom you ask. I'm going to defer to Procter & Gamble (P&G), which must be doing something right if they've become the world's largest advertiser. P&G would say that despite the bewildering complexity of digital media, their job as marketers has not fundamentally changed; in fact, it continues to be simple. Their job is to understand consumer behavior and create big ideas. P&G is imploring the industry to fall in love with ideas all over again.

There's a reason why the digital tail is wagging the idea dog – the advertising industry is infatuated with new. Digital is the proverbial shiny object, and in their zeal to be seen as cutting edge, agencies are quick to embrace the newest rage in electronic media. No matter that it may not be the right medium for the message, it's the right medium because it's the new, new thing in a business that loves new.

You'll have to decide which approach is right for your business. In the meantime, I'm going to take my dog out for a walk and see if we can find some tails wagging their dogs. Haven't had any luck thus far.

TARGET VALUES
TO CREATE VALUE

S ince marketing begins with targeting, most marketing is dedicated to demographics. With this approach, a target audience is defined, expressed, and measured numerically, beginning with age.

In addition to the age-based approach of targeting, other models look for relevance in a consumer's life-stage. This approach is based on the premise that consumers develop new and unique lifestyle needs as they enter into new life phases (eg. a young mother's first baby).

Each of these models – age and stage – dominates today's marketing, but they have inherent limitations when applied to the aging consumer.

Age is a very tempting way to target aging consumers. However, the logic of this rationale typically breaks down in practice in one of two ways. First, targeting a group of consumers by using a common metric like age makes the assumption that the age-based cohort is monolithic; in other words, all of the consumers are the same and will act the same. This approach flies in the face of what we fundamentally know about Boomers — they are a collection of individuals who celebrate their differences and defy mass definition.

Second, being age-specific is tempting because it's usually a neat and tidy solution for organizing a brand's offerings. While this approach may work in some categories – especially those where product and packaging nomenclature is complex – more often than not it has a stigmatizing effect. Aging consumers know they're aging but they don't want to be explicitly identified by a chronological age.

The logic of stage-based targeting is equally as compelling. While understanding the new needs that emerge at new stages of one's life is absolutely essential, how that understanding is leveraged in marketing is critical. In speaking to a consumer's new stage, one must be very careful not to overtly signal that the consumer has an age-based need. Stage-based promises are okay as long as the stage does not imply age.

Given that the traditional age and stage-based targeting models pose issues for targeting aging consumers, there's need for a new model: generational marketing. In this model, one markets to consumers' generational values — personal beliefs that endure irrespective of their age or stage. Generational values guide behavior and brand choices, and when you truly understand them and can tap into them, you can make authentic connections that help your brand genuinely improve the consumer's life.

The inspiration for this model comes from a sociological approach called "generational cohort theory", which maintains that events, social change, and pop culture affect the values, beliefs, attitudes, and ultimately the behavior of individuals. In this framework, a generation is less about the age of the group and more about their shared experiences, especially those from its youth.

When executed well, a message inspired by an understanding of the target consumer's values is almost always going to result in more authentic, effective communications. Authenticity is critical, given that Boomers are not only the Most Valuable

Generation™ in marketing, but also the savviest and most experienced consumers. This is true by virtue of the fact that they have been on the receiving end of more media and more messaging for longer than any other target. They are going to hold your brand to a higher standard, not because they are cynical, but because they demand more from the brands they have loved for so long.

In summary, if personal values are core to one's being, then they need to be core to your efforts to influence choice and improve peoples' lives with your products and services. This is especially true, if not essential, with an aging consumer whose values have been well defined over time.

MAKE SURE
YOUR MARKETING
HITS "HOME"

The largest, wealthiest generation in history is now retiring at a rate of 10,000 per day, a trend that will continue every day for the next 15 years. The better part of the nearly 76 million Baby Boomers are now in the process of "reverse commuting" – shifting their daily focus from the workplace to the home-place. As the hours that were once spent commuting and at work are reallocated to the home, the dynamics of how the home is used and how lives are lived within it will undergo sweeping changes. This shift is an opportunity to market products and services that align with newly emergent needs and desires of a home-centric lifestyle. Google's purchase of home systems innovator Nest Corporation for a reported $3.3 billion is just the "tip of the iceberg" and the latest indication that the remigration to the home-place is a real marketing power trend. When a high-tech software company such as Google decides to invest billions in home-based consumer technology, they must believe that the market for these products and services has a great deal of room to grow.

This trend will manifest itself in many ways, beginning with the house itself. If there's no place like home, then imagine what it feels like to live in a newly renovated home. The typical Boomer home has evolved from a comfortable nest that once nurtured a growing family to a space that is in transition. The prospect of more time at home is triggering a desire to alter the home in a way that nurtures the inhabitants' dreams for their future. It is time for the "Me" generation to rediscover aspects of their lives interrupted by family and work demands in the years prior.

Data from the National Association of Home Builders shows that 73% of buyers aged 55 and up don't want a second-floor master suite. Boomers wishing to save their joints and avoid stairs have helped fuel this trend. First-floor bedrooms and bathrooms, wider doors and hallways, better lighting, bigger windows, and easy-to-maintain exteriors and landscaping are becoming common.[65] After years of paying others to do what they did not have time to do themselves, many home-centric Boomers are getting back to being do-it-yourselfers (DIY). What was once a chore has become a source of enjoyment – made possible by improved home and hardware products now readily available from DIY retailers.

Space vacated by grown children is being repurposed to support the passions of Boomers. The home is being transformed into a space to entertain others and to enjoy quality friendships in a comfortable setting. Whether a sewing room, man cave, or home office, the way in which home space is used is being transformed, and because the endeavor is driven by passion, Boomers are spending considerably more to convert living space into lifestyle space. For the more affluent, expect renovation and expansion on a grand scale.

Next, consider that a healthy home is a happy home. One of the most important aspects of aging is "liberation". Typically this feeling is triggered by a shift from the structured demands of the workplace to a more flexible post-work lifestyle. Liberation is characterized by the ability to focus on life priorities that were previously sacrificed to the priorities of work and career.

Natural Marketing Institute (NMI) research indicates that Boomers are taking more personal responsibility for their own health.[66] As such, "healthcare at home" is being redefined – not with their parents' medical equipment, but with mobility-enhancing products, technology, and devices that provide at-home solutions. Active Boomers will seek and pay a premium for products that work without calling attention to an age-related disability.

The NMI research also indicates that more than half of Boomers indicate their biggest fear of aging is "restricted mobility or difficulty getting around", up from 44% in 2006. Mobility will be the greatest new high-order benefit, and exercise and diet will be integrated into a virtuous circle for more aging Boomers. Expect Boomers to purchase home exercise equipment and establish home workout routines to stay fit and feeling great.

As they return to the home-place and re-nest for the next phase of their lives, the passion for protecting the environment and sustainability has become a worthwhile and enduring value for the majority of Boomers. This belief is on the rise. More than eight in ten Boomers think we live in a wasteful society and are trying to save and reuse as much as possible. Three out of four care about products that use recycled materials.[67] As such, they will be inclined to invest some of their wealth in creating homes that make sustainability easier. The Boomers are in the best financial position of any generation to spend money on rebuilding, recycling, and retrofitting their homes for a sustainable lifestyle. Implications for home improvement retailers, homebuilders, contractors, and manufacturers include the rapid growth of active and passive solar energy systems – now standard features in many new homes and renovations – hyper-insulation, geo-thermal heat pumps, composting areas, and systems that capture, store, and reuse rainwater.

As they came of age in the 1960s and 1970s, many of the Boomers were self-identified as activists. The Civil Rights Movement and Vietnam War helped give rise to a generation that adopted and supported political and social causes. The passion for the environment that was stoked then never went away. It has matured alongside the Boomers, who now have the time, money, and maturity to understand that environmentalism begins at home.

Finally, more than a few Boomers will be coming home to a full house, not the empty nest they may have dreamed of. The share of Americans living in multi-generational households is the highest it has been since the 1950s. Boomers have become the latest "sandwich generation". The trend toward multi-generational living – gathering momentum since the 1990s – has been accelerated by the combined pressures of a systemic economic contraction, depressed housing values, an uncertain employment picture, the inability of many families to find affordable childcare, and an overall devaluation of retirement savings. With Boomers' parents moving in and the kids not moving out, many Boomers will find themselves managing an even more demanding home dynamic.

This will provide marketers with the opportunity to address a multi-generational home as a household as opposed to a collection of separate and distinct consumers. This unique household composition will affect a plethora of industries, from consumer packaged goods to transportation to travel, and will have an obvious impact on housing.

So sweep off the welcome mat and leave the front door open. Marketing's Most Valuable Generation™ is coming home to the place they value more than any other. The Boomers are back to where it all started, and they're getting ready to start all over again.

If you're marketing to age, it's time to make sure that your efforts hit home. Virtually everything bought in a grocery store, a mall or the web lands in the home to be used there; in essence, home is where most brands live and it's also where the Boomers are going to get down to some well-earned living. The "work hard, play hard" generation is catching its breath and getting ready for what comes next, and the next phase will fundamentally involve the home. The most important generation in the history of marketing is about to experience the most dramatic lifestyle change since they were married and started families decades ago. Change begets opportunity, and now is the time to put the home at the center of developing new products, services, experiences, and messages for the new aging consumer. It seems that there really is no place like home after all.

USE THE RIGHT TOOL
FOR THE JOB

M y grandfather, a New England dairy farmer and proprietor of common sense, always used to say, "Use the right tool for the job." It's pretty simple advice that's stuck with me for a lifetime and has found practical application from the workshop to the workplace. Yet, as fundamental as this instruction is, it boggles the mind how often it's either forgotten or ignored. If you're taking on the challenging task of marketing to age for the first time, this is advice you won't want to overlook.

The basic principle of this adage is pretty simple. The execution of a task is enhanced and simplified by the use of a tool, and it's the worker's job to determine which tool(s) is ideally suited to completing the task as intended. If this is so basic and obvious, why is it so often disregarded in the workplace?

In all likelihood, one of three things is happening. Either the organization lacks the right tools, the resources needed to access the necessary tools, or the workers *think* they're using the right tool when actually they are not. All three of these missteps are common when marketing to age.

No matter how sophisticated most marketing operations are, there's a good chance that they lack the right tools for marketing to age either because they haven't done it before, or because they're new to it. Imagine a mechanic (we'll call him Mike) who has spent his career working on cars and is now being asked to fix a motorcycle. While he's capable of the new task, he won't be able to start or succeed unless he does a few things first. Specifically, he'll need to learn more about the differences between cars and motorcycles, and he's going to need to get his hands on some specialized motorcycle tools.

Continuing our analogy, imagine if Mike's employer ("Deals on Wheels") either doesn't have motorcycle tools or chooses not to invest in them. No matter, he still wants Mike to repair the motorcycle, and since Mike wants to keep his boss happy, he resigns himself to using the car tools to try to fix the motorcycle. His instincts tell him that this is probably not the best course of action, but since he doesn't have a choice, he proceeds with confidence.

Now imagine that it doesn't even occur to Mike that working on motorcycles requires different tools than cars. He's inclined to think that since they're both vehicles, with many of the same functions and parts, that they're more alike than not. He's eager to fix the motorcycle so he can impress his boss with his mechanical diversity.

In all but one of these scenarios, our well-intended mechanic is either going to fail to fix the bike or he will fix it improperly. The successful scenario is the one that has Mike and Deals on Wheels planning the work and working the plan together. They diagnose what needs to be done, assess the available knowledge and resources, and acquire what is necessary to complete the job successfully.

Now, while you may be thinking that this silly little analogy begs the obvious, think again. The fact is that way too many marketers start the task of marketing to age thinking it's the same as marketing to consumers aged 18 to 49. Like Mike the mechanic, they don't see a meaningful difference between the car and the motorcycle, so they proceed with using the wrong tool for the task and the job gets botched.

The tools that are available to most marketers to age are likely to be the tools that the marketing organization has identified as part of a best practice or process that was optimized for the 18 to 49 age cohort. For the sake of this discussion, let's focus on consumer learning tools, specifically those used to gain consumer insight and those used to evaluate and validate concepts and communication.

If you're marketing to age, your insight-generating tools will need to focus on dreams and desires, not problems and needs; embrace values, not just behavior; differentiate between the irrational and rational aspects of aging, and capture that which is unspoken, which is where truth in aging usually lies.

Your evaluation and validation tools will need to use a sample that is age-precise (eg. 50-68 not 35-49 or 50+); deploy a creative stimulus that has been carefully crafted for an aging audience; be sensitive enough to get at the nuance and subtlety that's imperative with age; and rely on an aging norm, or in it's absence, judgment.

As Horace Greeley, founder and editor of the *New-York Tribune* (1811-1872) once said, "Common sense is very uncommon." Using the right tool for the job is common sense, but in the case of marketing to age, it's application is quite uncommon. Getting better with age begins with getting everything you need to do the job successfully, beginning with the right tools that are apt to be new tools.

QUALITY MATTERS

We frequently acknowledge that the Baby Boomers are the savviest consumers in marketing simply by virtue of the number of years that they have been on the receiving end of that which Madison Avenue has been selling to them. They aren't cynics of advertising per se, it's just that they've had a lot of practice sorting through well-intentioned messaging some of which resonates and some that misses the mark completely.

The best way to contend with their deep experience is to play to their strengths – their desire for authenticity. At this point in their lives, they're fatigued by salesmanship and they're simply looking for brands that "get" them – brands that understand what they want and are offering honest products with sincere messaging. You're not going to win them over by blowing a cloud of smoke in their general direction.

To an aging consumer, the most important element of authenticity is quality. By quality, we don't simply mean something that is expensive or luxurious; instead, we're speaking to their desire to have things that are made the way they used to be made. You see, the Boomers have been witnesses to the continued degradation of quality over the course of their lifetimes. Products that used to be made to last a lifetime are now manufactured overseas at lesser quality, not simply to be cost competitive here in the U.S., but to build earlier obsolescence into the business model – if your jeans wear out faster, you'll be back in the purchase cycle sooner.

Still further evidence of this degradation is the erosion in value that is driven by package or count downsizing. To an aging consumer, it seems as though everything is getting smaller and, as if that's not bad enough, it's simultaneously getting more expensive. At the rate that some of these brands are going, one has to wonder if they will continue to downsize themselves into non-existence. Quality is heading toward the edge of the cliff.

In response to the aging consumer's desire for authentic quality, we're starting to see a number of savvy brands that are stepping up with premium merchandise. We're also seeing the return of brilliant marketing nomenclature like "vintage", one classic word that evokes traditional quality without suggesting that the Boomers themselves are out-dated. No one is doing vintage quality better than Filson, a purveyor of durable clothing founded in 1897 to provision the Yukon Gold Rush. They were founded on the premise of rugged durability and they have stayed absolutely true to that heritage for well over a century. Their quality has not wavered one bit over that time and when they recently realized that their pricing was out of range for the younger consumer, they doubled up their efforts on the Boomer consumer for whom their value equation is spot on. The Boomers value enduring quality *and* they have the disposable income to afford it. Filson's advertising message says it all: "From one generation to the next". The implication here is that "we're still making quality the way our generation always has, and because of that, you'll be buying something worthy of passing on to the next generation". Filson isn't just selling quality, it's offering timeless durability.

Believe it or not, when I talk about brands like Filson who have nailed their value proposition by re-framing it with Boomers, there's inevitably someone in the audience who questions whether an aging consumer – the one who's running out of life – would actually invest in something meant to last a lifetime. For unenlightened folks like that, I can't write this book fast enough.

So in the end, if you're marketing to aging consumers, you'll want to be sure that you're offering them a strong value that is driven by authentic, enduring quality. This is the generation that's already lived a lifetime, but it's intent on living another one. They've experienced quality for decades and they know the genuine article when they see it. This is a generation that has both choices and the power of choice and it's almost certain that they are going to opt for those products and services that are as enduring as they are.

LIVE FAST,
DIE OLD

The expression "live fast, die young" has been part of popular culture for some time, perhaps beginning as the title of a film directed by Paul Henreid in 1958 and perpetuated by the memorable Eagles lyric that immortalized James Dean as being "too fast to live, too young to die (bye bye)".

You don't hear many older folks saying "live fast, die young" – no, it lives in the province of heady youth who fear age but not danger. The gist of the expression is that old age is so unpleasant that one is better off dying young. Oh and by the way, if people live fast now, they're going to cram a heck of a lot more fun into their lives before they die young. Well, I guess that's one way to live your life.

One of these days I'm going to put 20 Baby Boomers in a room and ask them what they think of these words of wisdom from the rebellious fringe of youth. Don't misunderstand me here – yes, we were them at one point, and while I never put those words in writing, I and the rest of my generation probably pushed the envelope a little too far at times. The point is, we're not young anymore, and we're not about to start living by someone else's rules or definitions. No, we have our own motto, and it's "live fast, die old". The translation of our expression is, "Live fast every day, and get even faster as you get older."

Earlier in this book, we had fun with the medical diagnosis of Boomeritis, the symptoms associated with engaging in physical activity that is inappropriate for one's age. Boomers think this is hysterical – it's a badge of honor to suffer from an injury resulting from an extreme activity that pushed them beyond the limits of what "the norm" says they should be doing for their age. It's a symbol of living fast, which is the only way to live when you're getting older, because it means that you're cramming more into every one of the limited number of days you have remaining in life.

When I was growing up, people used to say that the great American dream was to live a better lifestyle than your parents. So I set out to own a bigger house in a better neighborhood, and when I was close to achieving the dream, I realized that I was chasing the wrong dream. I was exhausted, and in my early middle age I was convinced that the new American dream was a nap. Now that I am a few years older, I've redefined the American dream yet again. This time, the ambition that fuels me is to sleep only when I'm dead, and I'm not alone in this. There is joy in aging and most Baby Boomers are quite proud of what we've achieved in our lifetimes, and we're brimming with competence and confidence. We're incredibly optimistic about our futures, futures that consist of a series of days, each lived better than the next one.

I suppose that I am guilty of discounting the wisdom of people who were older than me when I was young (remember "don't trust anyone over 30"?). My father's favorite lament – which I think was meant to be advice – was, "There aren't enough hours in the day." I can remember rolling my eyes as if to say, "Dad, get over it." Now I have become him, and not only are there not enough hours in the day, the hours that I do have are racing by faster. Have you ever wondered why older people get up earlier and earlier as they age? They'll tell you that it's because they can't sleep as long anymore, but the truth is they're trying to cheat time by making more time in their days. As I write this, it's 5:15 am – you get the point.

Since I'm a Boomer and I'm never going to admit that I'm "running out of time", I'll offer you a different confession: "I'm living fast and I'm planning to die old." They say that youth is wasted on the young. If the young really think it's better to "live fast and die young", then there may just be some truth to this saying. I just hope they'll slow down a bit so they can survive youth and be able to speed up when they get old.

LUCK IS
A STRATEGY

You've heard it said before that luck is not a strategy. Translation: merely hoping that things will turn out as planned is an insufficient plan for success. Mostly true, but maybe not.

I've worked with many brilliant creatives over the years, but I will never forget one particular writer's words of wisdom back in the '80s. Clearly they've stuck with me all these years. In the aftermath of a particularly frustrating client meeting – one in which everyone was overanalyzing the research results and prescribing "paint-by-number" creative solutions – the agency copywriter admonished the client by telling him that he had to "give luck a chance to work". Everyone on the agency side shot him steely looks, and the client raised three eyebrows. What on earth was he suggesting? Everyone knows that luck is not a strategy – did he not get the memo?

It took me 25 years of experience and reflection to eventually realize that what he was saying was brilliantly insightful. By saying "give luck a chance", he was really saying that if you consistently do things the right way, success will eventually come to you in ways you could not have planned for.

Business is full of success stories based on positive, unintended consequences: 3M's Post-it Note™ or the manufacturing malfunction that led to Häagen-Dazs' distinctive, firm texture.

More recently, I came across two inspirational stories from two of the most famous purveyors in the New York City restaurant trade: Pat LaFrieda and Danny Meyer. Each has had their share of "luck" in becoming massively successful.

In his new book, *Meat*, LaFrieda tells a story of the early days working in his family's small butcher shop on Leroy Street in New York City's Greenwich Village.[68] Late one Friday, when most butchers had already closed for the day, he received a call from a distraught young chef who was desperate to get his hands on a loin of veal for that evening's dinner course. Pat promptly offered to cut him one, and as he was leaving the shop to deliver it, his father asked him what he was up to. When he explained, his father lectured him about his naivety: "Everyone knows that no one cuts meat for chefs on a Friday – the only reason he's calling you is because every other butcher in the city has cut off his line of credit." He went on to explain that his misguided son was going to lose money on this client, but Pat took the meat to the chef anyway, claiming that there was something about this new chef that he liked, some gut instinct that was telling him that taking care of this guy was the right thing to do.

When he arrived, he learned that the chef had ordered a veal loin from his regular butcher earlier in the week, but had been shipped a rack of veal instead. By the time he discovered the error, it was too late, and the only butcher who came to his rescue was LaFrieda. The young chef was none other than Mario Batali, a wildly popular chef, restaurateur, and media personality in America today – who subsequently used his own fame to put LaFrieda "on the map", enroute to becoming the most celebrated butcher in America.

Danny Meyer, one of the most successful restaurateurs in the world, has been in the news lately with the recent initial public offering for Shake Shack, his hamburger mini-empire with 63 restaurants worldwide and ambitions (and now capital) to expand to at least 450.[69] With all the $1.6 billion hype over his premium, flattop grilled burgers, everyone's forgetting that Shake Shack began as hot dog cart some 14 years ago.[70]

What LaFrieda and Meyer have in common is that they are consistently brilliant in their core offerings of quality and hospitality, respectively. When you can work from a strong foundation of fundamentals, you give your instinctual choices a better chance to succeed. This is how "luck" succeeds.

As marketing to age is a relatively new phenomenon, you're not going to have ready access to proven fundamentals or best practices. Instead, you'll have to rely heavily on your instincts, and you'll need to do so at a time when many process-driven marketing cultures are suppressing the role of judgment and instinct.

Branch Rickey once quipped, "Luck is the residue of design." His full quote includes additional inspiration: "Good luck is what is left over after intelligence and effort have combined at their best. Negligence or indifference are usually reviewed from an unlucky seat."[71]

You'll need a strategy for marketing to age and it needs to begin with sound intelligence and strong effort. Once you've done that well, you'll be guided by your instincts, knowing that luck is probably riding on your shoulder.

MAKE HUMAN CONTACT: REPLACE ONLINE WITH ON-LIVE

I just had a "live chat" with an AT&T service representative that was great, were it not for the fact that neither of us spoke a word. Apparently, 25 minutes of texting now passes as a "live" conversation. Go figure.

"Live" has been leaving marketing since advertising first replaced the door-to-door salesman in the 19th century. Print was the original surrogate for live, to be later supplemented with electronic media that became the standard of advertising communication for most of the Boomers' lives.

Then came the digital revolution, and with it, a blistering pace of unthinkable innovation that has permeated our world. The physical terrain of our lives is giving way to a landscape that is astonishingly virtual.

The examples are too numerous to list, but just think about the end-state of marketing, the essence of why we do what we do: triggering a purchase. That purchase used to involve a trip to a physical store, where you were greeted by a live salesperson who influenced your decision. When you purchased an item, you pulled paper legal tender from your wallet, put it in the teller's hand, and got a handshake on the way out of the store. By contrast, how much physicality or human contact is involved in purchasing a dictionary (one with a new definition of "live") on Amazon?

I'm not suggesting that we go back to the "good old days" – no, they're good and gone and change is mostly good. Instead, I'm encouraging you to stay grounded in the essence of the human experience, particularly as you embrace the aging consumers for whom the above scenario was – and still is – the desired modus operandi for purchasing goods and services.

Arianna Huffington, president of The Huffington Post Media Group, says it best: "Though digital is at the center of our world, live is more popular than ever ... the need to actually be live and connect with human beings and listen to people in the flesh seems to be the paradox of our age."

At the risk of getting existential, think about how digital communication has changed interpersonal interaction and the essence of human relationships. Forgetting about the fact that too many people walk through their days with their heads down staring at their mobile devices, how about the new ways that we manage conflict? Sadly, it's a lot easier to share bad news with a significant other or co-worker when you can draft it on email, revise it until it's perfect, and then just hit send. Yes, "live" is leaving our world every time we allow humanity to be stripped out of human interaction.

Arianna Huffington's words are suggesting that it's best to zig when everyone else is zagging. Imagine what an impact you could have on an aging consumer by replacing that which has become virtual about your product and its purchase experience with what was once physical. Zappos, a US-based online retailer of footwear and related fashion merchandise, has done this brilliantly with the perfect balance of virtual and physical: you get the ease and convenience of ordering shoes with a few clicks, but because they make returns so easy, you get to spend time handling, eyeing, and wearing your new shoes. The initial purchase is made online, but the ultimate purchase is made on-live – in the home, the consumer's physical world.

One of the recurring themes of this book (behold the power of repetition) is the need to communicate to the aging consumer with authenticity. That new dictionary I just bought defines communication as: "The transformation of information, thought or feeling so that it is satisfactorily received and understood."[72] I have encouraged you to avoid selling by telling and to instead do it with feeling, feeling that comes from a place of genuine consumer understanding.

As the Boomers age, they are placing less of an emphasis on acquiring things and more on availing themselves of experiences. A trip to Greece to see the Mediterranean live is a much more meaningful aspiration at this point in their lives than a new car.

As you begin to explore the ways in which you might be able to put more "live" into aging consumers' lives, don't underestimate the power of real. We're talking about the Baby Boomers here, the generation that sang from the hilltop to let the world know that their Coca Cola was the real thing, which years later we now know meant *we're* the real thing, and we're never going to change.

LEARN SOMETHING NEW FROM ANCIENT WISDOM

arketing tends to be so preoccupied with the newest new thing that it seldom looks to the past for inspiration. If marketing to age is the current trend for future growth, then we would be wise to look back in time for the wisdom that we'll need to guide us on the journey forward. Looking back is critical, as it allows us to leverage the experiences of those who have already done what we have yet to do.

Now to be clear, we're not talking about best practices here – we're talking about ancient proverbs. There's a reason that these common sayings are still so common thousands of years later; it's because they are based on universal and timeless truths. Who doesn't quote Lao Tzu's, "A journey of a thousand miles begins with a single step" at least once a year? It's eternal because its message is incredibly clear, but not always obvious.

This book is brimming with advice for *how* to market to age, but it's just as important to know how to *start* marketing to age. Complicated? No worries. Lao Tzu had it all figured out back in 550 BC. The best way to get started is to get started (why does that sound like Yogi Berra's attempt at Taoism?). As basic as that advice is, it's the most relevant wisdom for the task. Despite the obvious upside in marketing to age, most marketers don't even get started because they're afraid to take the first step on a journey that will take them somewhere they've never been before.

Let's see if we can't learn something new from a different piece of ancient wisdom – a proverb from Roman philosopher and politician Cicero (106 –43 BC): "Big things have small beginnings." This is well suited when considering marketing opportunities as massive as marketing to the aging consumer.

How could Cicero have known that marketing to age was the next big thing? Obviously he didn't, but apparently he did know two things: one, that big things are intimidating, and two, that you can't reap the benefits of something big unless you play. Incredibly clear, but not always obvious.

A small beginning for marketing to age could take the form of sizing up the prize and identifying the key consumer issues for your category. How many Boomers wear sunglasses and how many of those use magnifiers for reading? If you walk into the typical sunglass outlet, you would be shocked to discover how few if any options there are for fashionable sunglasses that have a magnifying element below eye level to help aging consumers read or type messages on their phones while active in the sun. This demonstrates a big opportunity that could be seized with a small beginning, as simple as the market survey just described.

So thanks to our wise Roman philosopher, perhaps we're now on our way toward realizing big gains in the Age of Aging. Now what?

Consider our friend Lao Tzu's perspective on the matter: "The farther one goes, the less one knows." If what you're after is truly big, it means that you're going where other marketers have yet to go or that you're doing things in ways that have never been done before. Exciting yet daunting at the same time.

One of the best consultants I've ever worked with – Garry Shelp – had great words of wisdom for the fear of dealing with the unknown. He would simply say, "You'll know more when you find out." Perhaps he was channelling Lao Tzu, because his message had a certain soothing quality to it. It was his way of saying it's okay to not know what you don't know, and that with a little bit of patience and good faith, things will become clearer as you proceed. It is brilliant in its simplicity and is advice I have practiced in all aspects of my life ever since.

Inherent in the wisdom offered by all three of these inspirational men is the concept of forward motion. All business is dynamic, because all business is opportunistic. It's common knowledge that the big rewards go to those who move toward big opportunities; the biggest gains go to those who do this first and do so with speed.

By definition, none of these ancient proverbs is today's news, but for those who are putting off big possibilities, they are as timely as ever. If you put these timeless words of wisdom into the context of marketing to age, they are deep with meaning, yet so basic in their application.

The Chinese teacher, politician, and philosopher Confucius (551–479 BC) had it right when he observed that, "Life is really simple but we insist on making it complicated." Nothing is complicated about taking a small step forward. Marketing to age is about marketing to the same people your brand has coveted for so long – take the next step with them as they move forward in time – this is not a leap of faith.

THE NEXT EMERGING MARKET IS NOT ON THE MAP

Investors and innovative companies have long been obsessed with emerging markets and for good reason. While growth was once a worthy objective, the new imperative is *fast* growth, and there are few better ways to achieve it than getting into new markets first. For years, the hottest spots on the map were underdeveloped economies such as Brazil, Russia, India, and China (the "BRIC" countries). However, growth in these markets inevitably slowed, and now the search is on for the next and newest emerging, fast-growth opportunities.

As with the BRIC example, the predominant perspective on emerging markets has been geographic. Even the epicenters of the eternally emerging technology sector have been given geographic monikers such as "Silicon Valley", "Silicon Alley", and "Route 128". So it's no surprise that as smart companies search for the next emerging markets, they are most likely to be looking in "places" rather than "spaces", or age demographics.

The bias that the next big, emerging markets will be places on a map is perhaps the most salient reason most enterprises have been slow to discover one of the most significant, underdeveloped, and uncontested market spaces in today's global economy. We live in the Age of Aging, and no other trend will shape lives, make markets, influence public policy, and affect human welfare more than aging. As such, the next big, emerging market is not geographic, it's demographic. It's also not foreign, it's domestic, which means it conveniently begins right inside your own borders.

In fewer than five years, half of the US adult population will be 50 or older. They will spend close to $3 trillion a year and dominate most consumer packaged-goods categories. Globally, people 65 and older will soon outnumber children under five for the first time in history, and countries like China already have 200 million people aged 50 and over. In parts of Western Europe, walkers and wheelchairs already outnumber baby strollers.

The aging demographic is an emerging market for two reasons. One, it has all the economic hallmarks of a geographically defined emerging market – it's underdeveloped, largely uncontested, and ripe with fast-growth potential. Two, most baby boomers that comprise the aging market have recently turned 50 or older, thus aging out of marketing's 18 to 49 sweet spot. Said another way, they have "emerged" from the 18 to 49 cohort and are now fully resident in a freestanding and fertile 50+ market.

John Maxwell, a global leader at PricewaterhouseCoopers (PWC), advises that it takes bold and fast-acting pioneers to win big in emerging markets. Maxwell posits that those who break new ground usually win if they have a taste for risk, the ability to disregard conventional wisdom, and a commitment to stay in it for the long haul.

Great advice, but perhaps PWC's chief economist and emerging markets practice head Harry Broadman sums up the risks and opportunities of emerging markets most succinctly with this admonishment: "The biggest risk in emerging markets could be just ignoring them."

While it's sometimes convenient to ignore advancing age, it's nonsensical to ignore global aging. Those who "break new ground" in the emerging market of aging will be joining the likes of a modern-day Gold Rush. The modern-day pioneers of business who get there first will find nuggets of opportunity in plain sight, while those who wait will find themselves digging for the leftover dust of a missed opportunity.

Rarely has a market opportunity this big been so "invisible", but the explanation is pretty clear: aging is the emerging market that's *not* on the map.

CONSUMERS DON'T KNOW WHAT THEY WANT UNTIL THEY DO

As much as we would like to think that our consumer-learning tools and processes are thoroughly effective in assessing consumers' needs, most are inadequate in their ability to address unexpressed needs. If these needs are real, and they are consistently not expressed, then there's a pretty good chance that there's a valuable, unaddressed market space waiting to be capitalized on.

Given that many of today's product categories are competitively mature, understanding the location of these uncontested spaces is more critical then ever. As such, we need to find better ways to either predict what consumers want or to coax them into expressing needs they didn't know they had. As an advertising colleague once said to me years ago, "If you can identify a need that consumers don't know they have, then only you can solve it for them."

Predicting needs, and encouraging the expression of the unexpressed, are really challenging endeavors. Predicting the future inherently involves trial and error, and error is not something that's encouraged in today's low-risk, high-return business context. Similarly, trying to get consumers to open up about something that their conscious mind does not acknowledge involves some deep psychology that's usually not within the purview of most market research capabilities. So if unexpressed needs and future requirements are critical to understand but we aren't good at understanding them, what's the answer?

To get the answer, let's start with a truth. Many consumers – especially those of age – don't know what they want until they do. Said another way, they are fully satisfied with the product they have until a better product comes along that delivers a benefit or solves a need that was not apparent to them in the context of the current category experience. In this case, all we know is what we know. We define the category on the basis of the way it's always been because we can't conceive of it being any different.

One of my more memorable agency assignments was the KitchenAid portable appliances business. At the time, the KitchenAid offices were located in a little schoolhouse in St. Joseph, Michigan, down the road and out of sight of parent company Whirlpool's global headquarters. I'm not sure where the "s" on appliances came from, as KitchenAid only made one product in one color – its iconic stand mixer. These mixers were so well built and beloved that they literally lasted a lifetime; we often heard stories of children squabbling over the inheritance of their mom's venerable mixer. Consumer satisfaction at its best.

KitchenAid stand mixers are used in kitchens. Kitchens had typically been functional workspaces where the head of the household labored over the preparation of a meal. When the mixing and the cooking was done, she would then present the meal to her family that was waiting on the other side of a swinging door that concealed the kitchen from the dining room. In that environment, the appliances on the countertop were tools, and users took care of the tools by covering them to protect them from dust (think white stand mixers with white covers).

A few years in, we noticed that American homes were undergoing a significant change. Now kitchens were being transformed from functional workplaces to the heart of the home. People were adding on to their kitchens and building "great rooms", places where family and friends could congregate and connect before, during, and after mealtimes.

When kitchens become the heart of the home, the things on the countertop became home furnishings. And if they were going to be home furnishings, then style and design needed to become equal, if not paramount, to function.

We brought this to life in advertising with a truly great theme line – KitchenAid: "For the Way It's Made." The line spoke to how well the product was made and how well the consumer could make great things, too.

That's when we asked, "Why don't we make these things in colors other than white? If they're being used as home furnishings, shouldn't they come in different colors?" To make room for new colors on the manufacturing line, we discontinued the production of dust covers.

Without deliberately intending to, we had also solved one of KitchenAid's business problems. The KitchenAid stand mixer was, and still is, incredibly durable. They don't break down. Once consumers buy one, they can keep it forever.

By offering the stand mixer in a variety of new colors, we were creating an obsolescence that hadn't previously existed. The new colors were so irresistible that Boomers "needed" to have a new mixer even though the current one was built to work for another 70 years. Out with the old, in with the new. This was the beginning of the Boomers' new definition of "disposable" income.

The mixer color initiative went so well that we soon extended it to a full range of kitchen tools — toasters, blenders, food processors, and coffee makers. In the end, we put the "s" in portable appliances.

In the KitchenAid example, none of these Boomers knew they wanted a new mixer until a new one was created for them. It became absolutely necessary to own another one in another color, as doing so helped the consumer to not only feel current, but to also make a home furnishing and culinary statement.

Another great example of something we didn't know we wanted was Apple's iPad. The technology behind the laptop computer and the smartphone was so brilliantly effective that it was virtually impossible to conceive of any incremental innovation that could improve the technology experience in any meaningful way. Technology had satisfied consumers beyond their wildest dreams. How could there possibly be any undiscovered space in this leading-edge category?

Make room for the tablet. Not only has it been widely embraced as a "must have" that you didn't know you needed to have, but its applications have spread beyond personal use to the retail sector, where it is quickly replacing the cash register (remember cash?) as a transactional device. While I scoffed at first, iPads have also replaced unwieldy and incomprehensible restaurant wine lists. Want a complex, brooding Napa red for $75 or under? Tap the search tabs and suddenly you have a wine list within the list. Out with the tome and in with the tablet. Who knew I needed a better wine list after all these years?

While all consumers find themselves wanting things they didn't know they wanted, this is especially true of the aging consumer. The progress of life perpetually presents new realities that impose new needs and desires, but as one ages and the remaining life span gets shortened, this dynamic gets compressed. We are capable of anticipating many things, but as we have repeatedly indicated, we suppress thoughts about things like aging that are discordant with our desired view of life. If we're not thinking about the new needs that aging will present, we're more apt to find ourselves needing something we didn't know we needed.

So this all makes good sense, but what can a marketer do to anticipate what the consumer can't anticipate for themselves? The KitchenAid and iPad stories are both examples of brands that created new needs by expanding existing needs. The mixer did not change, it just got a new paint job. The iPad was not new, it was simply a larger iPhone. At their core, both are examples of simple innovation, but their impact was dramatic. In the end, you don't always need to anticipate or predict the next new consumer need. If you constantly seek to understand and expand the need you currently own, you will be able to extend your brand into spaces that the consumer is willing to go because in actuality, you won't really be asking them to go that far. Innovation can be an intimidating word. Done right, it is not transformation, but simply about transportation to a neighboring place that feels familiar, even if it isn't.

GO BEYOND BRAND LOYALTY TO BRAND BELONGING

In my first book, *The Old Rush*, I talked about a new state of brand loyalty that I call "brand belonging". This way of thinking was inspired in response to a query that I hear often: "Is loyalty dead?" Most often, this question is directed at employment (is the employer-employee contract null?), or relationships (what's with the escalating divorce rate?), but what about brand loyalty? You know, that coveted state of marketing ecstasy where consumers love you so much that they buy your product or service again and again. It's probably fair to say that it's not dead, but it's definitely under siege.

In military strategy, if one is under siege, they can either dig in and defend their territory; retreat and regroup to fight another day; or relocate to higher ground to seize back the advantage. If you're a marketer, the first two options are usually intensive and costly endeavors. Ideally, it's best to move to higher ground to enjoy a position that your competitors can't readily attain.

In my years at Saatchi & Saatchi, we espoused a belief about branding that was called "Lovemarks". This was an attempt to create a new, higher level of loyalty to rise above the traditional level of loyalty that was under siege. It spoke to a type of loyalty – "loyalty beyond reason" – that was theoretically less impervious to switching.

That cutting-edge theory of loyalty is now more than a decade old, and in those years we have witnessed unrelenting pressure on loyalty, accelerated by a lingering global recession that prompted unprecedented levels of value-driven brand switching. At the same time, the Most Valuable Generation™ of consumers – and arguably the most loyal – aged out of advertising's 18- to 49-year-old sweet spot. There's never been a better time for a new philosophy and approach to brand loyalty.

We are about to see the advent of a new model of brand loyalty, which we call "brand belonging".

Brand belonging is a philosophy that begins where loyalty leaves off – engagement – and goes further, to a level of relationship that is nearly permanent. Loyalty simply means a consistent and dedicated pattern of choosing a brand. Belonging says the brand is so meaningful to me that I have become one with the brand. The brand is essential to my being. It defines me. It is part of me. I cannot live without it.

Take Harley-Davidson. It's not a motorcycle; it's an ethos. When you buy a Harley, you don't just buy a means of transportation, you join a community. To own a Harley is to belong to Harley – it is instant kinship. Harley riders recognize each other on the road and form instant friendships based purely on the respect and trust derived from ownership. While Harley nurtures the heritage and ethos that it has built up around its bikes, the vibrancy of the Harley ecosphere is equally driven by the passion of the riders who are members of the distinctive Harley clan. Harley and its owners co-perpetuate belonging.

Loyalty programs, done well, can become belonging programs. In my mind and heart, I am not just loyal to Delta Airlines – I belong to Delta. So profound is my loyalty that I will literally opt for a higher-priced connecting flight on Delta over a cheaper, direct flight with another carrier. The others are just carriers, but Delta is my airline.

With the nearly universal dislike of air travel, how could something so wonderful happen? Simply put, Delta has found a way to personalize a commoditized experience for me. As proof that the little things can make a big difference – especially in a low-satisfaction category – it brings me great joy every time I board a plane and the flight attendant says, "Hello Mr Hubbell. Welcome back – thanks for your miles and your loyalty." How much does it cost them to say that? Nothing. How much does it mean to me? Priceless. Oh, and by the way, I'm a business traveller, which means that I fly frequently and frequently pay full fare. They love me, and I love them. We belong together.

Lou Pritchett, a legendary P&G salesman and change agent, once defined the objective of loyalty as one of "keeping the costs of switching high". It's a very interesting way of thinking about loyalty at a time when most think that success lies in keeping costs low to keep prices low. The "cost" that Pritchett was speaking about is the value that the consumer associates with the benefits of the brand. If you can keep the value of the brand experience higher than the competition, the consumer will have a disincentive to switch because doing so will result in a forfeiture of value.

Brand belonging is a relationship-based strategy that perpetuates loyalty by keeping the costs of switching high. Once you've had a taste of the "good life", it's hard to go back.

Finally, in a day and age where social media advocacy plays such an important role in shaping brand reputations, consumers who feel like they belong to your brand is like money in the bank. They aren't just Facebook friends, they're part of a club – "belongers" are the ultimate brand ambassadors.

Thriving in the Age of Aging is all about striving to do things differently. That begins with embracing the highly valuable aging consumer, but it also requires challenging the ideology around core topics like brand loyalty. If the Boomers believe that they're going to live forever, then so do you. It's time to set your sights on a loftier ambition – it's time to go beyond loyalty for a relationship that will last a lifetime.

LOOK FOR TRENDS WITHIN THE TREND

T rend seekers are so intent on setting the trend that they often overlook significant trends within the trend. Many times, these subtrends end up being more lucrative than the broader trend that precipitated them.

In *The Old Rush*, we looked to the discovery of gold in California for inspiration. While many prospectors struck it rich by finding gold, the true, sustained wealth of the Gold Rush came not from gold but from the products and services created to support this emerging industry.

Brands that persist to this day had their origins in the Gold Rush. A Bavarian immigrant named Levi Strauss made canvas pants durable enough to stand up to the tough work of mining; John Studebaker manufactured wheelbarrows for the miners and went on to build one of America's great automobile fortunes; James Folger created pre-ground, pre-roasted coffee for miners who were too busy for the task; and two enterprising businessmen named Henry Wells and William Fargo provided banking and shipping services to miners who previously had no way to store or convert their nuggets into cash.

While each of these entrepreneurs made fortunes in different ways, they all shared the same approach: they made money by going to where the money was. The money today is in aging, and if you want some of it, you'll need to get to where it is, and get there first.

There are three prominent trends within the macro trend of aging – simplification, self-improvement, and discovery – which flow from the Boomers' focus on wellbeing, joy, and growth.

The Boomers are in a new stage of enjoying an easing of family and career responsibilities. When something as central to one's life as home and work are simplified, the ripple effect is profound. They are simplifying and streamlining their assets, resizing homes, and enjoying a daily lifestyle that is markedly less complex than their midlife years. As they get more and more of a taste of the joy of simplicity, many of them are wondering why they were so fixated on asset accumulation all of their lives. They are less materialistic and quality of life has become the new must-have acquisition.

As part of their focus on personal growth, they're finding pleasure in self-improvement. This begins with physical health and wellbeing (yoga or pilates anyone?) and runs the full range of the human condition to include emotional, intellectual, and spiritual growth. The most highly educated generation in history have become lifelong learners and are streaming to classrooms and campuses across the country, giving new meaning to "continuing education". *Time* magazine recently called them the "Holy Enrollers", as according to the Association of Theological Schools (ATS), the 50-or-older group has grown from 12% of students in 1995 to 20% in 2009, the most recent year for which data is available.[73]

As one continues to age, the novelty of doing new things (to avoid the monotony of old things) further gives way to a determination to do new things to defy the momentum of aging. The irrationality of aging has Boomers believing that perpetual vitality is possible and that keeping their bodies, minds, and souls engaged and energized is the prescription for longevity.

Lastly, the Boomers have always been an experiential generation, born with a passion to discover. As they age, the "bucket list" effect has them feeling ever more eager to go places and do those "must-do" things. At the same time, their simplified lifestyles have created more discretionary "me" time. As they anticipate having more free time, 67% plan to spend more time on their personal hobbies and interests. They have more time to do the things they want to do before they run out of time. If you're in the travel and leisure space, this trend is clearly your friend.

Simplicity, self-improvement, and discovery: three high potential micro-trends that only skim the surface of the deeper possibilities inherent in aging. For most first-time marketers to age, there's immediate growth for the taking simply by showing up and doing business in a largely uncontested market space. If you aspire to sustained long-term growth in aging, go beyond aging by looking more deeply at the trends created by the initial trend. With a generation as large and as lucrative as the Boomers, a mere ripple will have the potential to magnify into a tidal wave of opportunity.

LIFE CANNOT
BE JUDGED UNTIL
IT IS COMPLETE

I t's human nature to compare ourselves to others and chart our own success relative to the accomplishments of those around us. I guess it's part of what makes us competitive, and competitiveness is often a good thing if you believe in Darwinist philosophies of success. If we're going to insist on rating our lives along the way, we should at least remind ourselves that life is not a sprint, it's a marathon, and as such, we cannot judge it to its fullest until it is complete.

Aging gives one the incredible ability of reflection, also known as, "If I only knew then what I know now." As I look back on my youth and my young adulthood, I have distinct memories of several people whom I envied, all for various reasons. We've all been there, right? You find yourself sort of wishing that you were a little bit more like someone else, and while you know that it's not possible, it doesn't prevent the wistful thinking. When we do this, we're admiring others but also judging ourselves. We exalt our heroes and put them on pedestals, which has the effect of raising them while simultaneously lowering ourselves.

I can't tell you how many times I have replayed these moments of jealousy, mainly because each of the three people that I envied passed away well before their prime. I was devastated at the time, but time has given these tragic events meaning.

We can only live our own lives, and no one, not even ourselves, should judge those lives until they are complete.

Young marketers considering marketing to age are making an evaluation. They have to consider all of the facts before them and weigh the risks and rewards associated with action. Whether they realize it or not, they probably aren't just judging the business opportunity, they're also judging the aging consumer. Not only are they judging them from the vantage point of youth, but they are also judging the aging consumer at a point in time in their own aging life. The young executive, like most of us, lacks the ability to project forward in time to judge what the life ahead will look like.

Marketers in this position can only do two things. First, they have to stop judging a life they have not lived, and second, they should defer to others who have been where they have yet to go. This advice is inherent in the premise of this book – the need to get better with the way we seek to understand age.

In summary, the Boomers have by and large moved beyond judging themselves within the context of others. Their life experiences have taught them the same lessons over and over, and high on that curriculum is the knowledge that we can only live our own lives. We have never been more self-aware or more confident in who we are. If you want to understand us, just ask us. We'll be happy to tell you what makes us tick as long as you don't judge us. You can judge us when our lives are complete, which is going to be a while because we've got a whole lot of living yet to go.

AFTERWORD

I wrote my first book to see if I could. The unfulfilled dreams of a lifetime tend to take on new urgency as one ages, so I figured out a way to conquer procrastination and managed to publish *The Old Rush*. As with most things on one's bucket list, I expected to check off the book thing and move on to the next enticing experience. Yet here I am putting the finishing touches on my second book, which I never thought I would write. The rest of my unfulfilled dreams were put on hold once again because a voice inside of me said that this book needed to be written.

In the two years since I wrote my first book, I have traveled the world to help clients truly understand the potential in global aging. Despite its staggering potential, it is still a largely misunderstood and underleveraged opportunity. So clearly, my work is only just getting started. When you fervently dedicate yourself to a task as I have, passion takes hold and at some point the task becomes a cause. It becomes a pursuit with such meaningful purpose that it subconsciously propels you in the direction of constructive change. Indeed, the right cause is like a seductive song whose power you can't resist even if trekking to Machu Picchu is next on your bucket list.

Getting better with age is a worthy cause, and this book is intended to be the provocative thought leadership that instigates positive change. Yet, even as I use the words "thought leadership", I hesitate because the term has been overused to the point that it has become trite and nearly meaningless. The notion of thought leadership first originated in a corporate context when coined in 1994 by Joel Kurtzman, then editor-in-chief of the *Booz, Allen & Hamilton* magazine. The intent of the term was to signal that leaders of organizations have the responsibility to inspire the thinking of others by sharing ideas that had merit. At the time, it was essentially a contemporary take on the traditional concept of "leading by example".

Many years later, the term is still used generously, but in a new context that has accelerated the dilution of its meaning. Because anyone can publish ideas on the internet, we are witnessing the digital proliferation of "thought leadership" in every possible shape and size. Are these self-publishers really generating content that's worthy of the distinction of thought leadership? Perhaps, but mostly I think not. At the end of the day, much of what is out there is simply thought, aspiring to be leadership.

The specific interpretation of thought leadership that inspired me to write this book is that of social mission combined with business vision. I reasoned that if those two things were grounded in a relevant need and articulated in an inspirational way, then I could well be affective in publishing thoughts that actually had the power to lead others to positive action.

Getting "better with age" is an ethical social mission. We live in the Age of Aging and no other force will do more to profoundly shape our world, our people, and the political and economic policies that sustain our quality of life. But for all its apparent obviousness, global aging is not getting the respect it deserves. It's an interesting idea, but it doesn't yet have the power to inspire action.

Getting "better with age" is also a strategically sound business vision. As investors demand stronger and faster results more consistently, emerging markets have never been more critical to success. For as long as global aging continues to be a largely uncontested market space, the aging consumer will surely be the next big opportunity for fast growth. While the business vision for global aging is just as compelling as its social mission, many businesses have been slow to act. On the business side of things, it would seem that we have the opposite dynamic at play – global aging is a powerful financial idea, but young leaders of enterprise presumably don't find the idea of marketing to old people to be interesting.

What compelled me to write this book was the need to express the global aging opportunity as true thought leadership. Not as just an admirable social mission or a lucrative business vision … but as both. I continue to believe that progress against such a worthy pursuit as understanding the implications of global aging has been slow because the world's age-inspired social ambitions have lacked a business vision, while business has lacked a vision to make the social responsibility of aging profitable. Look at what sustainability has become. The social mission to improve our planet began to prevail when businesses found a way to get the consumer to pay more for environmentally responsible products and practices. Positive change triumphed because the social and business aspects of global warming coalesced to create a win-win for all.

I don't pretend for a second that this book can change the world; but I do believe that it can start that change. The world will be a better place when we treat age with the same respect and admiration that we bestow on youth. Imagine what it would be like if we looked beyond physical appearance and found beauty in the wisdom of elders … if we felt obligated to recognize them all for all that they've done to create meaningful lifetimes for others. We can do more than just imagine, because the first step is an easy one – each of us can start within our own social spheres, and those of us in positions of broader influence can think about leveraging our scale to do the right thing.

If the world is to truly get better with age, then it's time for true thought leadership. I encourage anyone with interesting ideas and the power of ambition to step up and embrace aging as a positive, worthy cause that is deep with purpose. I implore readers to be more than just advocates who publish content, because we all know that actions speak louder than words. Lastly, I ask you all to listen for what others can't hear: that little voice inside each and every one of us that relentlessly speaks for what's right, even when doubt and fear try to silence it. It seems to know that our true potential is never fully realized, that we can always get better, and our best has yet to come. We are being called today, because today is the best day to move in the direction of the future.

RECOMMENDED READING

For those of you who are interested in further exploring the themes and topics discussed in *Getting Better With Age*, here is a select list of some preferred sources of research and insight.

Baxter, Richard A. M.D., *Age Gets Better With Wine: New science for a healthier, better and longer life.* Chicago, Board and Bench Publishing, 2002.

Cheung, Edward, *Baby Boomers, Generation X and Social Cycles, Volume 1: North American Long-waves.* Toronto: Longwave Press, Expanded edition, 2007.

Clurman, Ann and J. Walker Smith, *Generation Ageless: How Baby Boomers Are Changing the Way We Live Today . . . And They're Just Getting Started.* New York: HarperBusiness, 2007.

Crowley, Chris and Henry S. Lodge M.D., *Younger Next Year.* New York, Workman Publishing, 2007.

Dalzell, Frederick, Davis Dyer and Rowena Olegario, *Rising Tide: Lessons from 165 Years of Brand Building at Procter & Gamble.* Boston: Harvard Business Review Press, 2004.

Dychtwald, Ken, *Age Power: How the 21st Century Will Be Ruled by the New Old.* New York: Tarcher/Penguin, 2000.

Ehrlich, Paul R., *The Population Bomb.* Cutchogue, NY: Buccaneer Books, Reprint edition, 1995.

Freedman, Marc, *Prime Time: How Baby Boomers Will Revolutionize Retirement And Transform America.* New York: Public Affairs/Perseus, 2002.

Foot, David, Brian Gable and Daniel Stoffman, *Boom, Bust and Echo: Profiting from the Demographic Shift in the 21st century.* Toronto: Stoddart, 2001.

Gillon, Steve, *Boomer Nation: The Largest and Richest Generation Ever, and How It Changed America.* New York: Free Press, 2004.

Heath, Chip and Dan Heath, *Made to Stick.* New York: Random House, 2007.

Howe, Neil and William Strauss, *Generations: The history of America's future, 1584 to 2069.* New York: William Morrow & Company, 1991.

Howe, Neil and William Strauss, *The Fourth Turning, What the cycles of history tell us about America's next rendezvous with destiny,* New York; Broadway Books, 1997.

Hower, Ralph, *The History of an Advertising Agency: N. W. Ayer & Son.* Cambridge: Harvard University Press, Revised edition, 1949.

Hudson, Frederic M., *The Adult Years: Mastering the Art of Self-Renewal.* San Francisco: Jossey-Bass, Revised Edition, 1999.

Ibarra, Herminia, *Working Identity: Unconventional Strategies for Reinventing Your Career.* Boston: Harvard Business School Press, 2004.

Jones, Landon, *Great Expectations: America & the Baby Boom Generation.* Charleston, SC: BookSurge Publishing/Amazon, 2008.

Kennedy, Dan S. and Chip Kessler, *No B.S. Guide to Marketing to Leading-Edge Boomers and Seniors.* Irvine, CA: Entrepreneur Press, 2012.

Leider, Richard J. and Alan M. Webber, *Life Reimagined: Discovering Your New Life Possibilities.* San Francisco: Berrett-Koehler Publishers, 2013.

Levine, Stuart R., *The Six Fundamentals of Success: The rules for getting it right for yourself and your organization.* New York, Doubleday, 2004.

Levine, Stuart R., *Cut to the Chase: and 99 other rules to liberate yourself and gain back the gift of time.* New York, Random House Books, 2007.

Martin, John and Matt Thornhill, *Boomer Consumer: Ten New Rules for Marketing to America's Largest, Wealthiest and Most Influential Group.* Great Falls, VA: LINX Corp, 2007.

O'Hara, Christopher B., *Great American Beer: 50 Brands That Shaped the 20th Century.* New York: Clarkson Potter/Crown Publishing/Random House, 2006.

Owram, Doug, *Born at the Right Time.* Toronto: University of Toronto Press, 1997.

Pauley, Jane, *Your Life Calling: Reimagining the Rest of Your Life.* New York: Simon & Schuster, 2014.

Rosenblatt, Roger, *Rules for Aging.* New York: Harcourt, 2001. (Award-winning essayist, journalist, author, playwright and teacher, Roger Rosenblatt, shares some of his observations about aging and gives memorable advice.)

Smead, Howard, *Don't Trust Anyone Over Thirty: The First Four Decades of the Baby Boom.* Bloomington, IN: iUniverse, 2000.

Walker, Michael C., *Marketing to Seniors.* Miami: 1st Book Library, 2nd edition, 2002.

Wallace, Paul, *Agequake: Riding the Demographic Rollercoaster Shaking Business, Finance, and Our World Paperback.* Boston: Nicholas Brealey Publishing, 2001.

ABOUT BOOMAGERS
THE BOOMAGERS MANIFESTO

BoomAgers is the first modern creative services and marketing communications agency for The Age of Aging. At BoomAgers, we believe that aging is the most potent global power trend of the next twenty years. No other force will have a more profound impact on global economies, societies and cultures than aging.

Founded by Peter Hubbell in 2012, BoomAgers has grown exponentially from its humble beginnings with a single client and one part-time employee. From the beginning, BoomAgers has been purpose-built to deliver unique expertise into the aging consumer. Our insights, strategies and creativity enable both established global brands and emerging companies to capture the full value of the massive but under-leveraged aging marketplace.

We believe that "it takes one to know one," and we are proud to be Baby Boomers. We take it as a core truth that there is joy in aging, and we have the passion and experience to express elemental human truths in ways that make brands and products irresistible. We are Boomers dedicated to Boomers – the new B2B.

We believe that "the secret to success is knowing the secrets, and as Boomers, our team has accumulated years of invaluable experience in top roles at major agencies.

We've been there and done that. We know where the creative bullseye is, and we get right to the point.

We are practical pioneers. We are motivated by a collective dissatisfaction with the way things are typically done at big ad agencies. We have our priorities straight, and we put the consumer first because the consumer is the ultimate arbiter – that's who buys our clients' products and services. We also believe that sameness in advertising never works. So, we work differently – a process that starts by attracting and inspiring the best people in the business.

We believe that innovation is different from frantic change. Innovation is what you do to solve your hardest problems. We believe that the hardest problem for marketers today is generating fast growth in a slow-growth market. We know from experience that fast growth is created by doing business where no one else is, or doing business differently – we are convinced that targeting the under-leveraged, aging consumer accomplishes both.

We are the Boomer experts. We are your opportunity.

NOTES

1. "Who wants to live forever? Why are people living longer?" *Royal Geographic Society w/ IBG*: http://www.rgs.org/OurWork/ Schools/Teaching+resources/Key+Stage+3+resources/ Who+wants+to+live+forever/Why+are+people+living+longer.htm

2. *Id.*

3. *Id.*

4. *Id.*

5. "Longevity: An introduction to aging science." *The American Federation for Aging Research*. http://www.afar.org/docs/ migrated/110930_INFOAGING_GUIDE_LONGEVITY_Web.pdf

6. *Id.*

7. *Id.*

8. *Id.*

9. *Id.*

10. *Id.*

11. Stern, Peter, Hines, Pamela J. and John Travis. "The Aging Brain." *Science: The World's Leading Journal of Original Scientific Research* (October, 2014). http://www.sciencemag.org/ content/346/6209/566

12. *Id.*

13. Greenhouse, Steven. "Pushing Back Retirement, And Not Always For Money." *The New York Times*, (March 12, 2013) http://www.nytimes.com/2013/03/13/business/retirementspecial/ pushing-back-retirement-and-not-always-for-money.html

14. "Study shows majority of Baby Boomers plan to age in place." *Independa*, (December 18, 2014) http://independa.com/study- shows-majority-of-baby-boomers-plan-to-age-in-place/

15. "About MIT Age Lab." *MIT Age Lab*. http://agelab.mit.edu/ about-agelab

16. Parker-Pope, Sarah. "Surprise path to better sex: hip surgery." *The New York Times*, (April 8, 2013) http://well.blogs.nytimes.com/2013/04/08/surprise-path-to-better-sex-hip-surgery/

17. "Quotes about living in the moment." *Goodreads.* http://www.goodreads.com/quotes/tag/live-in-the-moment

18. "Is fifty the perfect age?" Harris Interactive Poll: (September 12, 2013) http://www.harrisinteractive.com/NewsRoom/HarrisPolls/tabid/447/mid/1508/articleId/1271/ctl/ReadCustom%20Default/Default.aspx

19. Hammond, Claudia. "Does life speed up as you get older?" *BBC's Future.* (July 10, 2012) http://www.bbc.com/future/story/20120709-does-life-speed-up-as-you-age

20. Greenhouse, Steven. "Pushing Back Retirement, And Not Always For Money." *The New York Times*, (March 12, 2013) http://www.nytimes.com/2013/03/13/business/retirementspecial/pushing-back-retirement-and-not-always-for-money.html

21. *Id.*

22. *Id.*

23. "Boomers 2.0. A Generation reimagined." *RLTV.* http://www.rl.tv/shows/boomer-initiative/boomers-20-a-generation-re-imagined/

24. Yu, Daniela and Julie Ray. "Boomers put more money than trust in banks. *Gallup.*" (January 21, 2014) http://www.gallup.com/poll/166979/baby-boomers-put-money-trust-banks.aspx

25. "Carpe Diem." *Wikipedia. The Free Encyclopedia.* https://en.wikipedia.org/wiki/Carpe_diem

26. "The Longevity Economy, Generating economic growth and new opportunities for business. A briefing paper prepared by Oxford Economics for AARP." *Oxford Economics.* http://www.aarp.org/content/dam/aarp/home-and-family/personal-technology/2013-10/Longevity-Economy-Generating-New-Growth-AARP.pdf

27. *Id.*

28. *Id.*

29. *Id.*

30. "Americans' Perspectives on New Retirement Realities and the Longevity Bonus. A 2013 Merrill Lynch Retirement Study Conducted in Partnership With Age Wave." *Merrill Lynch Wealth Management.* (May 6, 2013) http://wealthmanagement.ml.com/wm/Pages/Age-wave-Survey.aspx (accessed May 15, 2013).

31. "Encore Career Choices: Purpose, Passion, and Paycheck in a Tough Economy." *The MetLife Foundation and Civic Ventures.* (November 29, 2011) http://www.encore.org/files/EncoreCareerChoices.pdf

32. "The Longevity Economy, Generating economic growth and new opportunities for business. A briefing paper prepared by Oxford Economics for AARP." *Oxford Economics.* http://www.aarp.org/content/dam/aarp/home-and-family/personal-technology/2013-10/Longevity-Economy-Generating-New-Growth-AARP.pdf

33. *Id.*

34. *Id.*

35. "California Gold Rush." *Wikipedia The Free Encyclopedia.* https://en.wikipedia.org/wiki/California_Gold_Rush

36. "The History of Wine." *Wikipedia The Free Encyclopedia.* https://en.wikipedia.org/wiki/History_of_wine

37. "Aging wine: Why People Age Wine and When." *VinePair.* http://vinepair.com/wine-101/guide-to-aging-wine/

38. "Domaine de la Romanée-Conti." *Wikipedia The Free Encyclopedia.* https://en.wikipedia.org/wiki/Domaine_de_la_Roman%C3%A9e-Conti

39. *Id.*

40. "History of Cheese." *International Dairy Foods Association.* https://www.idfa.org/news-views/media-kits/cheese/history-of-cheese

41. *Id.*

42. "The Manufacture of Cheddar Cheese." *Wikipedia The Free Encyclopedia.* https://en.wikipedia.org/wiki/Manufacture_of_cheddar_cheese

43. "Cheese Making. *Wikipedia The Free Encyclopedia*."
https://en.wikipedia.org/wiki/Cheesemaking

44. *Id.*

45. *Id.*

46. Heffner, Dr. Christopher L. "Chapter 6: Section 2. Memory and Forgetting." *All Psych*. http://allpsych.com/psychology101/memory/#.VcS4VbeIC9Y

47. *Id.*

48. *Id.*

49. *Id.*

50. Chant, Ian. "You Remember That Wrong: Brain Distorts Memories Every Time You Recall Them." *The Mary Sue*. http://www.themarysue.com/memory-distortion-in-brain/

51. Tartakovsky, Margarita M.S. "The Power of Stories in Personality Psychology." *PsychCentral*. http://psychcentral.com/lib/the-power-of-stories-in-personality-psychology/

52. "Ford F-Series." *Wikipedia The Free Encyclopedia*.
https://en.wikipedia.org/wiki/Ford_F-Series

53. "Dragnet (franchise)." *Wikipedia The Free Encyclopedia*.
https://en.wikipedia.org/wiki/Dragnet_%28franchise%29

54. *Id.*

55. "Age and Happiness. The U-bend of Life." *The Economist*. (December 16, 2010) http://www.economist.com/node/17722567

56. *Id.*

57. *Id.*

58. "Marketing's Most Valuable Generation." T*he Nielsen Company and BoomAgers LLC*, (2012). http://boomagers.com/sites/boomagers/files/Boomers_-_Marketing%27s_Most_Valuable_Generation.pdf

59. *Id.*

60. Lafley, A.G. and Roger Martin. *"Playing to Win: How Strategy Really Works."* (Cambridge: Harvard Business Review Press, 2013)

61. Lafley, A.G. and Roger Martin. *"Playing to Win: How Strategy Really Works."* (Cambridge: Harvard Business Review Press, 2013), 3.

62. Gonzales, Laurence. *"Deep Survival: Who Lives, Who Dies And Why."* (New York: W.W. Norton & Company. 2003), 280.

63. "Marketing's Most Valuable Generation." *The Nielsen Company and BoomAgers LLC,* (2012).http://boomagers.com/sites/boomagers/files/Boomers_-_Marketing%27s_Most_Valuable_Generation.pdf

64. *Id.*

65. "Aging In Place Remodeling." *National Association of Home Builders.* http://www.nahb.org/en/consumers/homeownership/aging-in-place-vs-universal-design/aging-in-place-remodeling.aspx

66. "Health & Wellness Trends Database® (HWTD)." *Natural Marketing Institute (NMI).* http://www.nmisolutions.com/index.php/syndicated-data/overview

67. "LOHAS Consumer Trends Database® (LCTD)." *Natural Marketing Institute (NMI).* http://www.nmisolutions.com/index.php/syndicated-data/nmis-proprietary-databases/databases-overview

68. LaFrieda, Pat. *"Meat: Everything You Need to Know",* (New York: Simon and Schuster, 2014).

69. De la Merced, Michael J. "Shake Shack More Than Doubles its I.P.O. Price in Market Debut." *The New York Times.* http://dealbook.nytimes.com/2015/01/30/shake-shack-more-than-doubles-its-i-p-o-price-in-market-debut/

70. *Id.*

71. Torok, George. "Luck is the Residue of Design". *Motivational Speaker: George Torok.* https://motivationalspeaker1.wordpress.com/2009/07/17/luck-is-the-residue-of-design/

72. "Definition of Communications". *Merriam-Webster's Dictionary.* http://www.merriam-webster.com/dictionary/communication

73. Newsome, Melba. "Holy Enrollers. Why Boomers Are Going to Divinity School." *Time Magazine.* http://content.time.com/time/magazine/article/0,9171,2043476,00.html